Do You Know What You Are Doing, Lord?

A Jungle Journey in Search of God

Carol Lee Anderson

Chosen Books
A Division of Baker Book House Co
Grand Rapids, Michigan 49516

Published by Chosen Books
a division of Baker Book House Company
P.O. Box 6287, Grand Rapids, MI 49516-6287

Printed in the United States of America

Library of Congress Cataloging-in-Publication Data

Anderson, Carol Lee, 1946—
  Do you know what you are doing, Lord? : a jungle journey in search of God / Carol Lee Anderson.
      p.   cm.
  ISBN 0-8007-9261-0 (paper)
    1. Anderson, Carol L., 1946– . 2. Anderson, Neil, 1944– .
  3. Missionaries—Papua New Guinea—Biography. 4. Missionaries—United States—Biography. 5. Folopa (Papua New Guinea
  people)—Missions. 6. Folopa language—Translating. 7. Wycliffe
  Bible Translators. 8. Anderson, Carol Lee, 1946– . I. Title.
  BV3680.N52A3   1998
  266'.0092'2
  [b]—DC21   98-21482

For current information about all releases from Baker Book House, visit our web site:
                    http://www.bakerbooks.com

To those who serve in hidden places

Contents

Acknowledgments

"N ever start a writing career by writing a book."

Whoops! Too late.

The popular author who offered this advice knew what he was talking about. By the time I heard it, however, I had gone too far in the process to turn back.

It started when my husband, Neil, and good friend Hyatt Moore co-authored a book about translating the Bible into the Folopa language of Papua New Guinea titled *In Search of the Source* (Multnomah, 1992). People asked me teasingly, "When are you going to tell your side of the story, Carol?" Neil and I laughed and I replied, "If I did, it would be a very different tale."

The final nudge came at the tri-annual Urbana Missions Conference in 1993, a gathering of nearly twenty thousand young people on the campus of the University of Illinois. I remembered that God has a sense of humor when Neil and I were assigned to speak at a seminar called "Working Together as a Married Couple." Rather than try to fool the young generation audience, which was impossible, I opted for openness about our struggles. In response a great number of women came to me afterward and begged, "Please write a book. We haven't

10 Acknowledgments

been able to find anything on the subject of the real live experience of women missionaries."

Although I got in way over my head with this book, I am grateful to the many who encouraged me to write it. Not only did it tell my side of our experience and provide information for would-be missionaries, but writing my story has been a way to verbalize and finalize a great work God has done in my life. It has made me sit down and ask myself, "O.K. what *has* God done for me?" The answers have been mind-boggling.

I am also grateful to all my family and friends who read the manuscript in its various stages and offered feedback, suggestions and encouragement.

To my now very literate daughter Heather, whom I taught to read and write but who sent me back to my desk to write major revisions, thanks for being willing to teach Mom.

Jane Campbell, my editor at Chosen Books, helped me gather my scattered thoughts and make the book actually say something. Her visions, affirmation and wise advice made all the difference.

Finally I am grateful most to God most high, who took hold of my hand for the duration of the task.

> For I am the LORD, your God, who takes hold of your right hand and says to you, Do not fear; I will help you.
> Isaiah 41:13

Into the 1 Jungle

"Therefore go and make disciples of all nations.
. . . And surely I am with you always, to the very
end of the age."

Matthew 28:19–20

Descending steadily through the mist, I could see tiny dwellings nestled snugly side by side along the serpentine ridge. Hundreds of antlike dots waved welcoming antennae wildly as they moved toward the only stretch of flat, open ground—a clearing just big enough for the small helicopter.

Closer and closer we were drawn magnetically down to the jungle village. With both excitement and dread, my muscles pulled in the opposite direction, trying to hold back the inevitable. Braced for the coming impact on hard earth, my life flashed before my eyes. I had thought there should be a bolt of lightning out of the sky about now announcing our arrival and transforming me from a weak young female to Godly Woman, the ultra-spiritual being, able to leap tall papaya trees in a single bound, more energetic than a speeding helicopter.

But I heard no voice from on high saying, "This is my special missionary couple. Listen to them." Instead, while my knees knocked, the words of the Australian government officer at Erave Patrol Post echoed in my head.

"The Folopa people? Oh, yes, a savage lot. We've had plenty of trouble with them. Cannibals, you know."

The official had responded matter-of-factly when my husband and I asked for information months before about these rain forest inhabitants of the Gulf and the Southern Highlands Provinces.

Was this the same me about to be dropped off with my family and left alone with these, I hoped, former cannibals?

I had heard missionaries tell of their experiences since my early teens. They were so impressively mature and saintly. *What am I doing here?* I asked myself, about to embark on this new life.

Racing rotor wings drowned out all sound. I could hardly let myself think lest I be completely intimidated by the huge task I was about to undertake. For the last two hours my thoughts had been thankfully lost to the fascinating shapes, colors and contours hundreds of feet below. They had been busy flitting along cliffs, dipping down into sinkholes and picturing exotic creatures hiding on bushy pinnacles. Now, snatched back to reality, I saw my final destination: an orange ribbon against dark green, flashing through patches of cloud.

A sea of eager faces swarmed at the perimeter of our landing site as the helicopter finally settled on the ground. While the engine roared and the blades continued to whirl, the villagers stayed at a safe distance, but I could tell they were anxious to surge forward and get as close as possible. As they shouted and jostled one another, the intensity of their body language told me that indeed these were a strong and forceful people.

"Better head for the house," the concerned pilot shouted in his North Carolina drawl. "They're going to swamp you!"

I looked at the crowds and envisioned swarms of people overrunning and burying us in a stampede of bodies. Shrugging off this picture, I unfastened the seatbelts and bent down to give instructions to our children, six-year-old Heather and Daniel, almost three, who was trying to disappear into my lap.

"Heather," I yelled, gulping with determination, "when we get out, stay with me. We'll walk up toward our house while we greet the people." I pointed to the edge of the clearing where the newly constructed log building stood.

I had hoped to smile and sound confident while trying to reassure them that this need not be as traumatic as I was sure now it would be. Heather's wide, apprehensive eyes stared back. Daniel held onto me, his head buried in my chest as we set foot on the ground.

"Don't be afraid. The people are just happy to see us."

I tensed for what would happen when we walked clear of the danger zone. Just as I had thought, the riot rushed forward. Multitudes of arms were thrust toward us from all directions, each with a dark hand waiting to be grasped in greeting.

"*Haiyooo!*" many shouted in wonder and amazement as they touched fair skin and light brown, straight hair for the first time. Faces pressed ever closer—faces with deep-brown, sparkling eyes above thick-lipped, white, toothy smiles. Faces all so different, yet somehow looking all the same. Wizened, wrinkled faces with stained teeth (or no teeth); gaunt, sickly faces full of sorrow and pain; tiny, dirty faces with runny noses, terrified at the ghostly pale color of the aliens who had arrived in a huge, noisy bird from the great unknown.

Unwashed bodies, foul breath, pig droppings and damp, earthy smells assailed my nostrils immediately. I faced the decision whether to hold my breath and avoid the inevitable, or breathe and accept my life as it was going to be. Breathing seemed the wisest overall choice.

All sound was meaningless babble—loud, unending babble. Mouths were moving, syllables pronounced in rapid-fire succession. *Is that really a language?* I asked myself. Exaggerated expressions and gestures were directed toward me as they smiled and chatted. *What could they be saying?*

Ahead of me, through the crowd of dark arms, legs and torsos clothed in brown bark-cloth, I spied a white shirt. As I advanced several steps up the slight rise, I found my husband, Neil, standing beside the house waiting for us with a broad grin.

"Well, did you meet everyone?" he asked with amusement in his voice.

Throngs of greeters were not unusual to him now since several weeks earlier he had come to build our house.

"I think I did meet them all," I replied wearily.

We walked together the rest of the distance to the front door. Behind me I heard the sound of the helicopter engine revving for its departure. The small aircraft had completed its mission shuttling our belongings into this remote spot in the jungle and was about to return to Ukarumpa, its home base and the main center serving Wycliffe Bible Translators personnel on this South Pacific island. With a sudden, painful awareness of isolation, I turned to wave goodbye as it eased into the air, turned and shrank slowly into gray clouds. As fog descended in its place, my imaginary umbilical cord was severed. Disconnection with the outside world was complete.

"Let me introduce you to someone important," Neil said, leading me over to a fierce but dignified-looking middle-aged man.

He was clothed in a faded red, knee-length piece of cloth wrapped around his waist. The bark belt that held it in place resembled a six-inch strip of curved, quarter-inch plywood stained dark brown and fastened with bark string. From his pierced ears dangled circlets of opossum claws, and around his neck a large, flat piece of shell hung from a bark string. Although his nose had obviously held some ancient decoration, evidenced by the gaping hole between his two nostrils, there was nothing now but space. Grasping my hand lightly in his gnarled hand, he pinched my fingertips and spoke several sentences, none of which was even remotely recognizable.

"This is the head man," said Neil.

The man smiled proudly and nodded his head, though I was sure he did not understand the language we spoke.

"What's his name?" I asked.

"I haven't heard it said. They just call him the *topo whi*, or head man," Neil replied.

Then Neil extended his arm to draw closer to himself a young man wearing a white, buttoned and collared shirt and long trousers. "This is the pastor, Yonape."

The young man smiled and spoke to me in Melanesian Pidgin. Neil and I had already learned to speak this simple trade language, which was used extensively in the Territory of Papua and New Guinea (the eastern half of the island of New Guinea).

"My village is Yankuri," he said, pointing to the west. "I speak the Samberigi language. I have been here three years so I know the Folopa language as well."

I was relieved to know that someone in the village was able to communicate with us. Already I imagined all the uncomfortable situations we could get ourselves into with our ignorance of the Folopa language and culture.

"*Koneo.*" I repeated their greeting over and over as my face muscles began to get fatigued from holding a friendly smile. With Danny hanging heavily on my shoulders and an eternity of handshakes and pinched fingertips behind me, the front door appeared, and with it, relief.

Heather had gotten to the house long before me, and now Danny scrambled anxiously inside to get away from hundreds of staring eyes. Neil set about to show off his handiwork. Though very unfinished, the house was impressive. Its rough, bark-lined walls were darker than

I had imagined, but I could see it would be homey when finished and adorned with my decorative touches.

I wandered around the piles of cardboard boxes, peeking into the rooms in a stupor. My brain was numb and I could formulate no plan of action other than to nod my head and repeat dumbly, "Nice." Vainly I searched for something to cue me on what came next.

"I'm hungry," said Danny.

Hmm, food. We would have to find something edible in the jumble of containers.

"Where's the bathroom? I want a drink of water," said Danny.

"Well, there's no bathroom yet, but I'm sure there will be one before too long."

I watched Neil, now returned to work, running in and out, tools in hand.

"We'll all have to be patient until we get the house finished," I added.

"Where are the storybooks? Can we start school now?" begged my anxious, first-grade daughter.

"Why are those people staring at me? Make them go away," Danny whined.

"I can't make them go away," I responded. "This is their village and they want to see how we live. We'll find some curtains somewhere in these boxes and then they won't be looking in all the time."

Squirming bodies of all sizes jammed against our windows and door as they vied for the best observation point. For now we would have to content ourselves being monkeys in the zoo—the biggest attraction that ever hit town.

I focused on the boxes once again. Where would I begin? What was most important? Food? Schoolbooks? Curtains?

A small, bark-caped figure pushed through the door and hurried to my side. With a wide, toothy smile and large, humor-filled eyes, she looked up into my face and clasped my hands in hers. I could not understand what she said, but with hand and body language I soon determined that we were neighbors.

"*Hįka wisi,*" I said with some small confidence. I had learned this *Good morning* greeting from a Folopa speaker before coming here, and now sought to show that I knew at least something in her language. (The squiggly mark beneath the vowel, called a cedilia, indicates that the word is nasalized, or pronounced through the nose.)

A look of open bewilderment followed. She recovered and pointed to a small child in the doorway about the same size as my son. The little girl smiled shyly as we focused our attention on her. Then the tiny woman, with exaggerated articulation, said the child's name: "Haddi So" *(Hariso).*

I repeated the name. She bit the back of a knuckle and giggled. The crowd responded in unison, "Eeehhh!"

Well, now I knew the name of at least one person.

Self-consciously I turned back to the boxes as my neighbor looked on curiously. I lifted a cardboard flap as if to begin the job of unpacking. A nose and pair of eyes closely followed my every move.

"*Aahhghfp.*"

I stifled a scream and tried to subdue my surprise and fright. Two enormous cockroaches had scrambled over my hand and down into the depths of the box. How I hated cockroaches, and I had to begin by confronting the two largest I had ever seen! I pushed the lid down, gulped and made my mouth curve up on the sides, dreading the moment I would be forced to open the flaps and face the uncertain contents of this box.

The women saw my reaction and stared in disbelief.

"Who Said Ee." *(Husele.)* My neighbor pronounced the word in the distinctive, throaty voice of one who has breathed the smoke of hundreds of cooking fires. She glanced up at me, then rolled her expressive eyes toward

the onlookers, obviously enjoying her role as mistress
of ceremonies before the delighted audience.

I repeated the word for cockroach, *husele,* and in-
wardly shuddered over the concept. Squirming, I wondered what they thought of someone who jumped out
of her skin at the sight of a tiny insect, and was sure I
detected mocking in their laughter.

Just then Neil reappeared.

"Isn't this the best piece of real estate?" he asked as
he whizzed through the house. "Right in the middle of
everything. Learning the language will be a breeze with
everyone speaking it all the time around us."

Suddenly I was reminded that my husband was an opti-
mist of the first order, not to mention a radical extrovert.
How perfectly he fit into the whole picture! He was not
in the least fazed by bugs, nor did he seem overly aware
of cultural differences and mistakes. The challenges that
for me were daunting trials only appeared to spur him
on to greater and more glorious accomplishments.

It had occurred to me before volunteering for this job
that it might be difficult and perhaps uncomfortable. I
had left my predictable world behind where I could plan
and perform at my best. But now that I was in the thick
of this new adventure, it was much harder than I had
imagined in my missionary fantasy.

"*Haiyooo!*" my visitor exclaimed, flicking a thumbnail on her front tooth.

I turned to see her examine a pile of bedding. She
caressed the blankets tenderly as she mumbled to herself and clucked through closed lips. Shaking her head
in disbelief, she grabbed my hands again. "*Sekę whį so.*"

Later I would learn that this meant "tusk woman," a
person with a lot of status.

The window-watchers were asking for details. After
the young mother had described the riches she had en-
countered, everyone hooted and howled, "*Haiyooo!*"

Wasn't it lunchtime? Shouldn't everyone want to go home for a while? *They should get used to us in a few days,* I thought.

Somehow we managed to clear the house of people. But morning, noon and night, day after day, people talked, laughed, pushed and played outside our house. Curious, open, amazed, boisterous onlookers hung around in shifts of no fewer than twenty and watched lest they miss any fascinating detail of our lives. They pointed and conjectured, analyzed and provided a news commentary for the newly arrived of the next shift. Wearily I wondered if we would ever live "normal" lives again.

I continued to unpack boxes. Slowly and with great caution, I held each item at arm's length and gave it a little shake as I watched for any unwelcome creature invading my space.

In the next few weeks schoolbooks were located, lessons begun, windows covered. The house was getting more and more livable.

"Danny, let's take a last trip to the outhouse before dark."

My son peered out the window to see who was standing around.

"Don't wanna go."

"Yes, you do, now come on."

"No. Too many people."

Both children backed away from the door.

"O.K. We'll wait until after dark."

"No. Too scary. Big spiders out there."

Shivers went down my spine as I acknowledged the correctness of this observation.

"Now it's raining. Don't wanna go out in the rain."

It was hopeless.

And it *was* raining. Without knowing it we had planned our first period of residence with the Folopa people right at the beginning of the wettest time of the year. Since the first day there had been a little sun about mid-morning, with drifting fog and low-hanging gray clouds on either end. The rest of the time it alternated between drizzle and tropical deluge. Heavy downpours discouraged us from walking around much in the village. Besides being kept indoors, we were fully occupied finishing the house and learning to live in this new environment.

The watchers, however, were not discouraged in their vigil. We recognized most residents from seeing them on the front porch each day. Hariso's mother became a regular visitor. Her small house was next to ours, a distance of only twenty feet. It was inevitable that we should become well acquainted, as the walls of our homes were made from thin bark, and most Folopa family life took place in the covered area in front of the house.

Faithfully my good-natured friend pointed to an ever-present pig and pronounced with large, rounded lips, *"Hupu."*

I would not soon forget this word, nor the phrase *Hale walapó:* "The rain is coming."

Fifteen years, I thought as I draped soggy, mildew-stained laundry over a wire in the living room. *What will it be like for the next fifteen to twenty years, living for months at a time with a people who are as strange and unknown to me as any I could imagine? And what about spiders, dirt, noise, isolation, inconvenience and the never-ending gloom of rainclouds?*

But an even more important question haunted me: *Where is God in all this? Will He be here to protect us and meet our needs?*

I had experienced some severe trials getting to this point. Would God go before us now and make the way smooth as He had promised?

Sunday was coming. In fact, this coming Sunday was Easter. How far away home was, with its fresh, blossoming trees after the drab winter months. New life springing from dark, dead-looking branches. Resurrection life demonstrated in natural symbol. There was nothing like that here. The jungle always looked the same. We woke up to fog in the morning, and more clouds rolled in later in the day to enshroud us almost continually in gray.

Friends and family far away were preparing to meet together for all the traditional events, starting with the sunrise service—that glorious symbol of power, hope and the reality of the resurrection—and ending with the evening service, in which believers rejoiced together in the grace of God.

There would be nothing like that for our family this Easter. The small church that was already in Fukutao village would see a motley collection of faithful members whose only knowledge of the Bible was through stories that the pastor had heard from other pastors in the neighboring language group. Sermons were preached in that other language because the pastor did not know how to present the difficult concepts and strange words of the Bible in the Folopa language.

I awoke very early Sunday morning when it was just getting light outside and lay for a while in the semi-darkness. The white mosquito net was as yet undisturbed after a night of barring crawling things from our sleep. Sheets, rather than the promised curtains, hung over the windows.

I could not resist the temptation. Perhaps today would be different.

Slipping out of bed, I crept quietly to the window. If there was nothing to see, I would crawl back, pull the covers over my head and pretend I had never hoped for just one morning of blue sky, let alone a full-blown Easter spectacular.

Neil joined me as we pushed the sheets aside, to behold a warm glow radiating from the eastern mountains. Holding hands, lumps in our throats, we beheld ranges we had not known existed until that perfect morning. The puffy clouds on the horizon reflected the beauty of soft pink, orange and lavender. Soon a golden ball began to rise boldly from its hiding place, filling the world with piercing rays of heat and light. Everything looked alive and vividly clear.

As the sun dawned, dark, misty shadows fled and a quiet answer to my deepest question began to form.

From Darkness to Light

> Even the darkness will not be dark to you the night will shine like the day, for darkness is as light to you.
>
> Psalm 139:12

"Carol, Carol, is that you out there?"

I knew my mother was squinting through the back door screen trying to make out the inert, blanket-wrapped form that lay on the cool summer grass.

"What are you doing? It's time for lunch."

"Oh, nothing," I replied dreamily.

I peered down through a part in the enfolding blanket at ants tripping along through blades of grass. Looking at the vast expanse of lawn, I pondered the extent of their tiny world. There was so much more than they could see and understand.

"Hey, this way to the dead beetle." I scooted one gently toward a possible lunch and probably broke three of his legs in the process. "Whoops. Sorry."

Slowly I unwrapped myself and headed back to the house.

As a chronic daydreamer I missed some of the details of what was happening around me. This was especially true in school, where my typical response to a teacher's question was "Huh?"

My family was a mixed-up, patched-together bunch that finally numbered eleven—one mother, three fathers (serially) and seven children. It was your basic modern American family, except that Mother was Australian (a fact that probably made it even more modern and American). In fact, I was born in Australia. My American serviceman father married my mother, a widow with one small daughter, shortly after the end of the second World War. After I was born we moved to the United States—Spokane, Washington, to be exact. There two more children were added to the family.

My father was a deeply troubled man after the war. Nightmares of screaming soldiers burning to death haunted him after the airplane he piloted crash-landed. He alone survived to battle the memories with large doses of alcohol. One day when I was five years old he left, just disappeared with no explanation. My mother heard nothing until the divorce papers arrived.

A couple of years after my parents' divorce, my father's parents asked if their grandchildren could come to California for an extended visit. During this time I saw little of either my grandparents or my father, who lived nearby. Maggie, the housekeeper, was in charge of our care.

When my grandmother died suddenly in her sleep, Grandfather was distraught. Convinced that her death was our fault, he sent our father to tell us we were being sent home immediately. He did not want to see us again.

We arrived back in Spokane to find a new stepfather in our home. He was a quiet man who also struggled with alcoholism. The next several years were full of conflict as a result. But while the other children in the family (three more joined the family in my teen years) did modern American things like fighting with each other, riding bicycles and watching the Mickey Mouse Club on television, I was content to quietly escape into daydreams, off by myself.

"Hey, are you sucking your thumb again, baby?"

"Bucky Beaver, where did you get those big front teeth and all those freckles on your nose?"

Hot tears burned my face. These standard taunts were excruciatingly painful to my extremely sensitive nature. All I could think to say in my anger was, "Yoouuu!" Nothing more original or clever ever seemed to come to me, though I longed to be able to retaliate. Verbal virtuosity was not my gift.

They could always make me cry no matter how hard I tried not to do it. Soon I was known as "the girl who cried at the drop of a hat."

"There's a hat, Carol, time to cry."

They teased and I complied. I hated this routine and determined each time not to let anyone make me cry ever again. But someone always did.

When I was thirteen, it was getting on toward time to grow up, but that did not look like an attractive proposition. Adulthood hunkered on the horizon like a hungry lion. Soon it would pounce and its teeth would crush me. Who would I be once I was swallowed up into the world of grownups?

"Mom, is there a God?"

I genuinely wanted to know if there was something beyond my current experience of life, or maybe even something for which I could look hopefully to the future.

"Of course there's a God," Mother replied.

Staring into the starry sky, I searched for a sign of God's existence. "If You're real, then where are You, God?"

One day an enthusiastic-looking man stood outside on the front porch when Mother opened the door to his knock.

"We're offering a free week of summer camp for kids in the neighborhood," he said, smiling as he handed her an application form.

The Salvation Army youth center was across the street, and even though we rarely went in, somehow we qualified for their summer camping program. My two brothers and I were quickly signed up for the second week in August.

It turned out to be a rough week. There were more "Bucky Beaver" and stupid freckle remarks from mean boys. I had kicked the thumb-and-blanket habit two years before, so this, at least, was no longer an issue. But the last full day of camp saw me once again in tears.

The final night I lay on a top bunk in the rustic wooden cabin wondering if God existed and if He was able to see everyone on the earth. I prayed a simple, desperate prayer there in the dark: *God, are You there?*

I had heard about God that week in the camp chapel services but did not understand anything. What was it they were talking about? I had walked down the chapel aisle to pray with a staff person when the opportunity was given. Afterward I waited for something to feel different, but it didn't. Did this mean God did not want me? Maybe He was not real.

Nor could my counselor offer much help with my burning question, "How can I know for sure that I'm really a Christian?" I had asked her this question hoping not to arouse too much suspicion. I thought everyone who lived in America was supposed to have been born Christian.

"Just pray and tell the Lord you want to be a woman of God," was her reply.

It sounded simple enough. To be a woman of God— what an awesome thought! So I gave it a try, prefacing my prayer with a few disclaimers just in case: *God, I don't know if You're really there. I don't even know if You exist. But if You do, and if You are there, I want to be a woman of God.*

Immediately a silent hand moved. A shroud of darkness was brushed aside and bright light filled my consciousness. It was still pitch-black in the tiny cabin, but somehow the room glowed with a warm and loving presence. Wrapped by a powerful security blanket of assurance and peace, real and much greater than anything I had ever experienced, I drifted off to sleep sensing that all my questions would find answers. There *was* something worth living for. I was going to be a woman of God.

The only friend I made that week was a girl my age named Charlene. "You must come to our church camp next week," she said. "It'll be lots of fun." She invited me persistently day after day.

So the following Monday morning I found myself sitting beside Charlene on a lumbering old Sunday school bus, headed for I knew not what.

During the chapel time I sat on the edge of my seat as the youth pastor talked about Jesus Christ. I could not remember if I had heard this before, but suddenly it all made sense. God was real. Somehow, from wherever He was, God looked down and saw little me, one among millions, and He loved me.

Not only that, but He had given His only Son, Jesus, who died as a sacrifice to take away my own sins and the sins of everyone in the world. All I had to do was believe in Jesus, who He was and what He had done, and I would receive a whole new life.

I thought back to the last camp, to the dark night when something remarkable happened as I asked God to make me a woman of God. He had been present in that cabin, filling it with light and assuring me of wonderful things to come. It had to have been the Spirit of God Himself! There my new life had begun and I had been born again.

The answers I had so hoped for in the dark cabin were now a reality. I had never known such joy. Life was going to be so good after this! I determined that I would be the best Christian who ever lived. I would try harder than I ever had to be good.

An additional feature at church camp that week was a stout Asian missionary pastor. I sat in the front row,

cheered by his bright smile and hearty laugh and mes-
merized by fascinating tales of spiritual heroism in foreign countries.

"Trudging up the muddy hill," he recounted, "the missionaries came at last to a village in the jungle interior.
They were tired and hungry, but they didn't stop until they
had preached the message of hope to the savage natives.
Hundreds received the grace and joy of Christ as a result
of faithful service to God by those dedicated people."

The image of courageous, victorious missionaries was
forever etched in my imagination. I heard Isaiah 9:2:

> The people walking in darkness have seen a great
>   light;
> on those living in the land of the shadow of death a
>   light has dawned.

Surely I had been in darkness and was now in the
light. Thanks to God, I would never be in the darkness
again. And any future I had ever dreamed of could not
compare to that of being a missionary.

"How many people in this room will go on to serve
Christ at the ends of the earth?" asked the speaker. "Of
the hundred teenagers here, there will be only three or
four, no more. Will you be one of those three or four?"

I could hardly wait to respond. *Yes, I want to be one,*
I said loudly in my head. Visions of tearful natives
flooded my mind. They were kneeling at my feet thanking me profusely for the Gospel message. I knew it had
to be this way. That was the way I had felt when I heard
the message of salvation. And God would be so pleased
with me, I was sure. Why, I could almost feel the warmth
of His smile as I made the commitment.

With this decision firmly under my belt, I had settled
the direction of my life twice within one week. I would
be a Christian, and what was more, I would be a mis-

sionary to some faraway people. If I had been joyful before, now I was delirious!

All the way home in the bus I rehearsed what I would say to my family. I would tell them about Jesus giving me something to live for, and they would be so happy for me. I imagined the whole bunch of them falling to their knees, repenting and asking God to do the same for them as He had for me.

After arriving home, I carefully chose the right moment to break my marvelous news. A shock wave reverberated through my body as I heard, "I forbid you ever to go to that church again."

Much later I could understand Mother's reservations. She did not like the sound of this sudden conversion. What kind of funny business could cause her daughter to get this excited, especially since little Carol had been so quiet and solemn all her life? All this enthusiasm was quite out of character and just a bit alarming. It made very good adult sense.

"And I want to be a missionary when I grow up, just like the man who spoke at the camp," I added, since it was now pretty hopeless anyway.

"You're not taking my grandchildren to the jungle. Don't you know jungle natives boil people in pots?"

I was shattered. Was my new life to end so soon? As I headed at full speed for my bedroom, the floodgates burst. Although I tried to hide the pain, I wept loud and long. My puzzled family shook their heads in disbelief.

"They're probably all Communists," my mother said to me as I lay on my bed and cried. "The nerve of those people, telling my daughter she's a sinner! There now, don't you worry," she said with disgust. "We won't let you go back to that place."

Of Ulcers and Uvulas

A man's steps are directed by the Lord. How then can anyone understand his own way?

Proverbs 20:24

Compliance was my middle name, but after all, I was thirteen years old. Rebellion just this one time was in order. Making sure no one could hear, I called Charlene on the telephone and whispered, "Can you have your church send the Sunday school bus to pick me up? But not in front of my house."

The next Sunday morning I left home quietly and walked down the street to meet the bus. Returning just before noon was a little more difficult. My siblings were all watching to see what would happen as I strolled up the front walk.

"I thought I told you not to go to that church," Mother said warily.

I nodded my head in reply. "Yeah."

Please, Lord, don't let her stop me, I prayed furiously.

Mother seemed to be pondering the dilemma of my quiet determination. Silence followed.

The next week the same scenario took place, but no questions were asked.

Eventually the bus no longer had to stop down the street. My family agreed that I had not joined a cult. Some of them even decided to come to church with me and later became Christians.

The months and years passed. Finally the day came when I had to make my first major decision. I knew that to be a missionary, I would have to go to college after high school. I applied to Seattle Pacific College and was accepted. What an adventure to be leaving home, traveling all the way across the state of Washington and doing something with my life!

Just weeks before leaving Spokane for college, I started to get acquainted with Neil Anderson, a young man who had been in the youth group at church. He was two years older than I and now a Bible and Greek major at Biola College in La Mirada, California. *There isn't a chance in the world that he'd ever be interested in me,* I thought, but suddenly there we were, staring into each other's eyes and asking the big question: Could this be love?

"I would never date a girl unless she was interested in a missionary career," Neil had said to me on our first outing.

Mentally I analyzed the meaning of his statement and decided this was a good sign.

I left for school in September filled with anticipation. But before long I was aware that I was not doing well academically. And as the months passed, I began to experience severe stomach pain and strange bouts of choking. The doctor suggested that stomach ulcers might be to blame. On top of that, I started having terrible nightmares. My grades went down even further and I ended the year deciding not to return. My big adventure had turned to failure.

Neil and I had corresponded all that school year. In June I left Seattle and returned to Spokane. Now that we were both home for the summer, our relationship grew even closer and it was not long before we decided to get married. He told me he admired my sincerity and openness and honesty. The future brightened and I put my troubles of the past year—and the immediate prospect of a college education—behind me.

Neil was pleasantly opposite to me. He fit neatly into my concept of the ideal man. He was strong spiritually, physically and mentally. He knew what he wanted and was ready to work hard for it. He was full of confidence and seemed boldly ready to take on the world. Since my life was characterized by fear and lack of confidence, we made a great pair. This had to be a union made in heaven! I grabbed onto his confidence and we set off together, marrying the following December, 1965.

The happily-ever-after was short-lived. Life with all of its problems did not take long to arrive at our doorstep. Because Neil needed to make some alterations in his educational plan, it meant changing schools and his major, and three more years of unsettled life. For reasons I did not understand then, living in a state of constant change was hard to tolerate. My expectations of marriage had been that life would become manageable. But each time we passed a stressful period, thinking the next would be easier, it was just the opposite.

Shortly after we married, I became pregnant. We had not planned to start a family for at least a couple of years. To make matters more difficult, I had all-day sickness for seven months. I was hospitalized twice just being revived from my constant vomiting.

"Mr. Anderson, I believe your wife hates children." The young doctor looked down his spectacles sternly at Neil and me in the hospital room. "The vomiting is caused by her psychologically trying to get rid of the baby."

I did not think I hated children, but a doctor had said it, so it had to be true. I felt very guilty, as if I had tried to have an abortion. Also hard to bear was the knowledge that our plans had changed again and it was my fault.

Life was always rushing ahead, out of my control. I was trying to be the person I felt I should be, to do the things I thought were right. But the bumps in the road came suddenly, with never enough time for me to regain my balance. Why was life so unpredictable? When would I arrive at the longed-for haven of being organized, spiritually mature and ready for anything God brought my way?

Our daughter, Heather, was born and life was settled for seven months before it was time to move again. Back in Washington Neil sought to finish his degree, with his major now changed to humanities, at Eastern Washington University.

"We're going to be missionaries eventually," we told our friends and interested others. For me the goal was always safely out in front, dangling like the proverbial carrot we chased to give our lives direction and meaning. Someday I hoped we would stop long enough to relax, think things through, make a plan and calmly and slowly move forward. Someday I would be mature, prepared, ready to handle crisis—in short, all the things I thought missionaries were supposed to be. I would enter God's service as bold and confident as my husband.

After three years Neil graduated from college. Seminary now seemed a logical place for someone with his theological bent and love for studying the Greek language.

We packed up and moved again that summer, headed for seminary in Oregon. Looking at the long-range plan, I thought, *What a perfect time to have baby number two!* A nice, safe, secure-sounding plan. Heather was two and seminary should take up three to four years.

Then, with our planned pregnancy well underway, Neil came home to announce, "Well, dear, guess what I did today?"

"What?" I expected to hear some interesting tidbit about my husband's new school experience.

"I dropped out of seminary."

"You what? Why?"

"I went to my Old Testament class and there was a test." He handed me the paper with the big red F on the top. I read the contents and gasped in horror.

"What kind of question made you answer, 'Milk, fruit, cereal, bread and butter'?" I asked, truly puzzled.

"I don't want to sit through Bible classes that I've already taken at Biola. It's as boring as learning grocery lists."

I couldn't believe this was happening. "But how could you? What about our plans?"

"I learned all this stuff before, I tell you. Sometimes plans just have to be changed. I think we must be ready by now to go to the mission field. At least let's find out."

I was stunned. What about the new baby seven months away?

"No problem. Now, what I want you to do is write to these three mission agencies that I'm interested in. Ask them for their literature. You know, principles and practices. Got that?"

Panic was beginning to rise. Had I reached a place in my life where I was ready to go into the world and teach people how to live their lives when I had not done a very good job on my own life? I had to stall for time, at least until I could see the path more clearly.

I decided to strategize. "Well, why don't we just write to one mission agency and see what they say? If we don't like that one, we can write to the next one." This seemed to guarantee that months and months would elapse before I had to face my fears.

To my great relief, Neil agreed to this plan.

Next came the decision of which agency to write to first. "How about Wycliffe Bible Translators?" I asked.

Why not? I reasoned. Six of one, half-dozen of the other.

I had not planned on Wycliffe's responding to my letter so quickly, but there it was, a whole packet of information. Neil was elated as he read the material. He literally could not sit down. He jumped all over the room, saying, "This is it! This is my dream come true. I want to be a Bible translator!"

It was exciting, the way standing on the edge of a cliff is exciting. I could not help but feel a chill run up and down my spine.

It may be a good thing for him, I thought, *but what about me? Do I want to be involved in Bible translation? Maybe it won't matter. I'm a mother. Maybe this organization will be interested only in Neil's abilities. It probably won't matter that I'm not quite of the same caliber.*

I tried to wrap these comforting conclusions around my frightened mind.

We filled in the preliminary questionnaire, sent it off, and in no time at all we were being invited to come to the Summer Institute of Linguistics (SIL) course at the University of Washington that June. They wanted us both to take the course.

I wrote a letter back trying to get out of it. Surely having a new baby gave me a good excuse. People did not really take these courses when they had small children, did they?

"Lots of mothers with small children take the courses," came the reply. "We feel you will do just fine." The tone was friendly and confident. They did not know me, did not know I was a failure. I had left college feeling like a disgrace to the academic community. How could I face graduate-level courses in linguistics?

There was only one thing to do at this point: worry. I was an accomplished worrier and decided to outdo all my past efforts.

I went to the library to find out what linguistics was and found nothing that would help. I tried reading some books on culture, but was put off after reading that, in parts of the world like New Guinea, there really *were* jungle natives who boiled people in pots. Whew! We won't show that one to Mother.

In the months to come, we moved back to Spokane. I could only hope the baby would be born by the May 22 due date. School would begin just three weeks later in Seattle.

I should not have been surprised that baby Daniel was five days late, which is almost a week, which meant only two weeks until school started. In that time we had to move out of the rented house, pack up and store everything and drive to Seattle.

This is where the worrying really caught up with me. Within the first few days after the birth, I was being treated for stomach ulcers again.

Everyone at our church was excited that we were going off to see if we could be missionaries with Wycliffe. They had generously underwritten our expenses and were confident that all would go well. Even as we pulled out on the freeway for the three-hundred-mile drive, I was asking myself, *What am I doing? I'm not ready for this.*

%&   %&

"I believe this is about the youngest baby we've had here, isn't it, Ilene?"

The veteran missionary teachers were comparing notes while I was thinking, *You'd better believe it. No one in their right mind would be dumb enough to take a course like this with a two-week-old baby!*

"Well, you certainly are brave," Ilene smiled sweetly.

I smiled back but was thinking, *You have no idea who you're talking to. I can't believe I'm doing this.*

The first night of homework found me in a panic again, but I was soon rescued by my husband. I understood not a word of the grammar lecture.

"Hey, this is easy. Nothing to it. Let me explain it to you again."

Together we pressed on. After a few short weeks, the courses were not only understandable but fun.

"What in the world is a uvular trill?"

I tried to make the strange noise we were learning in phonetics class. It sounded like someone being strangled. *Are there actually places in the world where people talk this way?*

During the final interview at the end of the summer, I smiled through clenched teeth as I waited for the selection committee to tell me all the reasons I was not fit for missionary service. I rehearsed them to myself; I knew them well. There would be no surprises.

"Carol, you wrote here on your application that sometimes you're busy and miss reading your Bible and praying. When you're a Bible translator, you'll be on your own. There may be no one to feed you or encourage you in your spiritual life."

I knew he was right, but did he know what it was like having two small children?

"I'll try harder," I said, genuinely intending to do so.

With this and other words of exhortation, the interview ended and Neil and I left the room. I waited for someone to find the misplaced paper that summarized all my shortcomings. Nothing happened. Were they blind? I decided not to question their decision and accept the fact that we were now members-in-training with Wycliffe Bible Translators.

ꗥ ꗥ

During those weeks of the SIL course at the University of Washington, the next steps to becoming Bible translators were laid out for us. After leaving SIL at the end of the summer, we would prepare for our Jungle Camp session. This began in November in Mexico and did not finish until early May of the new year. That sounded scary. It was a good thing I had not known about Jungle Camp before this, or I might not have come. But if I could learn linguistics, maybe I could do the Mexico phase, too.

"Say, did you hear about the couple who drove through

Mexico and went off the road?" someone asked. "Yup, their car was all smashed up. Terrible."

"No, I didn't hear about that one," I replied as a shiver went up my spine.

"You have to watch out for those bandits who hide along the side of the road. They'll take everything you own."

"Oh, thanks. I *will* remember that."

"Take lots of insect repellent because you know the mosquitoes are ferocious. Of course, that won't stop the army ants from coming right through your shelter."

"You'll think the cockroaches are going to carry off the whole kitchen!"

"I saw this tarantula in the village . . ."

That really did it for me. I felt my stomach juices starting to stir into ulcer mode.

O Lord, You got me this far. You have to get me through Jungle Camp.

I prayed, but visions of tarantulas were now dancing in my head.

Jungle Woman

When my spirit grows faint within me, it is you
who know my way.

Psalm 142:3

 osquito nets."
"Check."
"Army surplus web belts."
"Check."
"Canteens."
"Check."
"Chocolate."
"Oh, no, you don't! You know
we can't take food items."

"Hey, I just thought I'd try. You know, for medicinal
purposes."

Finding and purchasing everything on the detailed
equipment list was a challenge. We tramped from surplus store to pawnshop, borrowed camping catalogs and
finally got it all together to fit conveniently into our used
Army duffel bags. We pushed and shoved, shoved and
pushed, and decided that packing for Jungle Camp
should be on the list of aerobic exercises.

We had been informed by veteran campers that taking
an old car into Mexico was a gamble. Whatever was

driven in had to be driven out again five months later, come what may. Despite the warnings, we decided to make the trip in our old Pontiac Tempest station wagon— a move we would later regret. But for then it seemed safe enough as we began the long journey that cold November morning of 1970.

We made our way down toward the border crossing in Brownsville, Texas. This was a great adventure for me, as I had traveled little in my 24 years. Heather would celebrate her fourth birthday in Mexico City, and Dan was just over five months old.

My plan was to shop on the U.S. side of the border for some food to take into Mexico. I wanted to make sure we did not have to buy much on the drive, as I had heard about the dreaded affliction people affectionately called *tourista* (diarrhea), which resulted when tourists ate local food of questionable origin. I am still not sure how this happened, but before I knew it, and before we had made any stops to purchase food, we found our-selves in a line of cars headed for the border crossing. I was in shock as we drove over the line and into the town on the other side.

I knew a little Spanish, but it did not seem necessary as Neil was doing quite well with his pantomimes and gestures. He got directions to a motel, which we quickly decided to pass by when we noticed a man siphoning gas from the cars in the parking lot. We drove on into the night looking for a safe haven.

We came at last to a small village and Neil remarked, "This looks fine to me." Then I saw a dark-looking man in a sombrero and handlebar mustache standing in the shadows. As he leered at us, I remembered the stories of bandits and desperadoes. Gripped by a fear that squeezed at my stomach, I stuttered, "N-no, not this one. Try the next town."

As we drove on, I grabbed an empty soft drink cup as a wave of nausea rose and I heaved. Each small town we passed had the same suspicious-looking character. I do not know how he managed to stay ahead of us! In each town I had the same fearful reaction: "Not this one." Heave.

Finally we spotted a motel with an American car parked outside. Must be safe. It was two or three in the morning and we were exhausted. After checking in, everyone slept peacefully except me. Someone, I reasoned, had to listen in case thieves tried to break into the car.

The American car turned out to belong to two young women also on their way to Jungle Camp. They were having a great time together and joyfully recounted their adventures to Neil. I felt so sick I wanted to do nothing but sleep, let alone hear about how much someone was enjoying this trip.

We spent the next night at an ancient manor house turned hotel. Suits of armor decorated the enormous hallway. Eating in the elaborate dining room proved too much, however, and I found myself again losing my dinner. But in the magnificent restroom behind ornate, hand-carved doors, I discovered too late that the water was turned off because it was not the tourist season.

The following day we drove into Mexico City, where the orientation part of the program was to be held. Because I had determined, for some reason, that nothing was safe until I reached a place where they spoke my kind of English, as we entered the SIL Center I could feel my whole body start to relax. After a wonderful cup of tea from the kindest woman I had ever met, I enjoyed relief at last from the nausea.

I had been about to pronounce this segment of my life a disaster. But after the three-day traveling nightmare, I returned to normal. Heather had her birthday with a real Mexican piñata. The orientation was fun, and we would soon be on the road again headed for the southernmost part of the country for training.

On the final leg of the journey, we drove accompanied by another couple who were also Jungle Camp–bound.

This proved wise, as our car developed mechanical problems high in the mountains just north of Cintalapa. Roger, our fellow traveler, drove ahead to find someone to tow the car into town. What he found was a mechanic only too willing to come and see what the problem was.

I knew we were in real trouble when I saw bits of car engine, which the mechanic had laid on the road, blowing away in the gale wind, just as the sun was setting. I realized somehow that we would get out of this one. But I had to admit it was going to be interesting to see how.

Our traveling companions ended up towing the car. The next morning the mechanic informed us that he wanted two hundred dollars to put the car back together again, and until he got the money he would keep all the parts in his shop.

If this had happened on the first half of the trip, I think they would have had to take me home in a pine box. We were in the middle of nowhere with no help in sight, but somehow my spirit of adventure had returned and fear had retreated.

We were rescued by a Wycliffe missionary who sent a taxi and tow truck to convey us the rest of the way. For the same price that the mechanic wanted, we found ourselves at the end of the line, San Cristóbal de Las Casas. Our car was put in the hands of another mechanic, who we trusted would restore its health while we shed all care and concern. We would not be needing it for many months.

Jungle Camp was a great experience. There was nothing bizarre or horrible about it. All the potential problems I had heard about never materialized.

Not that I did not still harbor some fear! In my first shower, in a dark little outdoor stall with a bucket of warm water swinging overhead, I imagined all sorts of bugs and spiders just waiting to spring from their hiding places. I could imagine their little faces grinning with evil delight to see this hunk of juicy flesh standing there with *Come-and-get-it* written all over it! That was all I could handle, and I took no more showers during the whole of the training. Swimming class in the river held a lot less threat for bathing. I noticed several women besides me who brought soap and shampoo.

Determined to succeed, I gave the training my best shot. Physical fitness, cooking, medical, mechanics, language learning—I enjoyed all the courses and felt I had done as well as anyone there. Then the evaluation came.

"Carol, some of the staff noticed there were times when your daughter was wandering around looking for you," the camp director told me. "Also, your son was heard crying while you were apparently busy with other things. We are confident that you're a good mother, but we want you to know that you mustn't neglect your kids just to get some extra duties done."

I made a mental note that the criticisms had come from the single members of the staff. Nonetheless I was aware that these people cared about kids. I would show them that I did, too. After this it would be kids first all the way.

The next step of training was called Advance Base. Here survival was emphasized. We had lectures and demonstrations on the how-to's. The final exercise, akin to no less than the initiation rite into Wycliffe, was the Survival Hike—the three-day event that inspired many a horror story and not a few SIL fun night skits. Here was the moment we had all dreaded. Even when the word was uttered, strong women fainted and hair stood up on the necks of everyone—that is, except my husband.

Neil could hardly wait. Not only was he already an accomplished outdoorsman, but he had made a hobby out of mountaineering and survival. He lived in hope that the unexpected and unusual would happen. Risk and danger brought out the best in him.

As he had often done, Neil now took me aside for a coaching session. He gave me careful pointers on how to make a survival shelter. I had already heard this in class, but he made sure I had the skills down pat. I got the impression he really did want me to return alive from this bush experience.

The moment arrived when the women were to leave on their hike. The men had already returned from theirs, and had lost no one to the jungle. That was encouraging. Sort of. We all marched out of camp as though we were being led to the gallows. It was very quiet.

Recreating a group survival situation, we all stayed together the first night and made a gang shelter. That was not too bad, although I noted confidently that we had some novices in the crowd.

The second night each woman went on her own to make a shelter in a different location. After picking just the right spot, I flew like a whirlwind to get done before dark. Once the light was gone, I planned to be inside of some kind of shelter, no matter what it turned out to be.

Before dark our staff leader came around to check on us. He said little, offered some help and advice, then went on to the next site.

As we were returning to camp on the third day out, I began to feel extremely itchy from head to toe. Later I counted more than three hundred bites from what I was told were "no-see-'ems." I hated the itching, but the fact that I never saw them was the better part of the experience.

It was finally over, and we all gathered to hear a debriefing of our total survival adventure. The staff leader reviewed the highlights of the men's and women's undertakings. Everyone had survived, even the women. We were all proud of ourselves.

Then he uttered words I would not soon forget: "On the women's hike, I noticed that Carol made a survival shelter that was actually better than her husband's. I don't know where she learned to do this so well, but congratulations, Carol."

It was the ultimate compliment—a soundbite that would play over and over in my mind. Neil was proud of me. I was proud of me. I had not failed.

This was the story that would eventually earn me the nickname "Jungle Woman" back at our home church. I never told them about my fear of the shower or throwing up much of the way through Mexico. What they did not know would not hurt them.

The final evaluation for that phase brought a different reaction.

"Carol, we noticed you were late for many of the lectures. We realize it is not always easy to get two small children ready, get them to the childcare shelter and get to the meeting on time. But we expect you to take your classes seriously and do the best you can to get the most from the training."

It was true. I had been late for meetings, trying to get my kids settled in the nursery. As I compared my two evaluations, I realized there was no way to get everything right. Sometimes my roles conflicted and there was no way around it. This was a dilemma—how to make everyone happy?

It appeared that there was no way to do everything right, no matter how hard I tried. How does one decide which is more important? Am I a career missionary who has children, or a mother who helps her husband to be a career missionary? This was but the introduction to one of many conflicts I would face.

The final phase of our training was called Village Living. We were assigned to live in an isolated village. The people spoke only the Tzeltal language, and it was our job to learn as much of it as we could in the six-week period. We were also expected to carry on the literacy classes that had been started by previous campers.

Boredom pushed me to the wall. Cockroaches and spiders unnerved me to the core. Literacy classes were the bane of my existence. I would not go bathe, as the locals did, in the stream beside our house. But some-how, at the end of the six weeks, I felt strongly that Neil and I were to continue on the path to becoming Bible translators. It could only have been the Spirit of God.

The fun was not over yet. We still had the long trip back up through Mexico to look forward to, in a car that we trusted was in one piece.

We began the trip. Chugging into Veracruz, we tried not to think about what we heard under the hood of the Tempest. I imagined bubble gum and bailing wire holding things together under there. *This ought to take some of the bounce out of Neil,* I thought as I looked the other way.

The accommodations were better in this scenic tourist town than those in Cintalapa. The mechanic was friendly and sympathetic. The diagnosis, however, was terminal: a cracked head and blown head gasket.

"Señor, there are no parts for this make of car in all of Mexico."

How had we overlooked such a detail in our planning? Neil was looking depressed by now. It was a somber evening. The thought of towing our car all the way to the border, paying for it and then getting back to Spokane felt like a wet, cold fog. Where was the light we needed to find the path again?

Neil got up early and went out to watch the fishermen prepare their nets. He prayed for guidance as the sun rose amid brilliant color and quiet calm. I lay in bed with a pillow over my head, not wanting to face the day.

Then Neil returned to the hotel room to make his surprise announcement: "I think the Lord wants us to get in the car and drive to Mexico City."

"Over one hundred miles, all uphill, cracked head?" I replied. "Why not?"

We had probably done dumber things. I was blessedly ignorant of the import of the mechanic's diagnosis.

We had already been through the most impossible situation I thought we would ever have to face. This was just one more.

The car started. That was the first good sign. The car ran—another good sign. There was no noise, no steam coming out the side. We drove and drove, waiting nervously, thinking any moment that it would be back to barely chugging along. Hours passed. We were still driving normally up the winding highway. We were happy campers.

Then, as we passed a sign that said *Entering Mexico City*, it happened. *Jerk, chug, chug.* Steam poured out the side of the car. Driving five miles an hour while angry drivers passed, shaking their fists at us for holding up traffic, we slunk down in our seats and pressed forward. Just a few miles to go.

Sighting the SIL Center, we were pushing the air trying to assist our dying vehicle: "Come on, you can do it, keep going!" After a second try at the driveway, we barely rolled inside the gate, our car breathing its last gasp. That was as far as that car ever went.

Getting out, I half-expected to see smiling angels hovering somewhere near the rear bumper.

There was still one major obstacle: the legal obligation we had to remove our vehicle from the country. We asked a knowledgeable person if there were any options for donating the car, and he pronounced the words we loved to hear: "It can be arranged."

Bearing an official document indicating the donation of one automobile to the Mexican government, we happily made our way to the airport.

Because our driver failed to notice the sign indicating the right turn-off, when we finally arrived we had to run, waving our tickets at the officials. But frowns turned to smiles when we presented the magic document—the car donation. Meanwhile, out on the tarmac, the engines were warmed up, the gangway had to be pushed out and the door reopened. We had managed to come very close to missing the plane.

But, I reasoned to myself, *how else would you expect an adventure like this to end?*

The training had accomplished its purpose. Even I could see that I had been stretched and had grown as a result. The Lord had seen us not only through SIL but through the field training phase as well. I bore a new determination to do the best I could on my work assignment, and to be a good parent above that.

I gazed out the airplane window as Mexico faded from sight, savoring each trial of the last five months. Surely all the big stuff was behind me now and I was ready for whatever lay ahead.

From the Mountaintop

The lot is cast into the lap, but its every decision is from the Lord.

Proverbs 16:33

As our airplane soared into the clouds, we joyfully left Mexico behind us. It was May, and in June a second summer of linguistics training in the state of Washington faced us. Then we would raise our financial and prayer support and depart for places unknown. Our motivation was the vision of giving the holy Scriptures, the Word of God, to a Bibleless people group. Behind this, of course: the conviction that this Book reveals the truth about God, and that truth changes people's lives.

SIL, the sequel, proved just as enjoyable as the first semester. Daniel was no longer an infant but a busy one-year-old. Heather, now four, was a great helper. I could sit back and advise those nervous first-year students with my own spine-tingling accounts of adventures in the jungles of Mexico.

With the first semester of classes out of the way, our orientation now included a detailed look at how a trans-

lation project proceeds. After choosing our Bibleless
people group and moving in, we would first have to learn
the language. To date we had taken courses on hearing
and writing the foreign sounds. We had learned how to
devise an alphabet scientifically and do the early stages
of grammar analysis. Teaching the people how to read
and write would come in there somewhere, then producing literature in the language. We would write papers, train teachers, produce dictionaries and, finally,
translate a minimum of the New Testament (and sometimes portions of the Old Testament as well) into the
language. And all this was going to happen in about fifteen years—the average time it took at that point.

A little mental calculation, and I had a picture of me
fifteen years from then.

I can do this, I thought.

The big dilemma now was, where in the world should
we go? We had to either ask for an assignment or take
whatever the committee chose for us. And the committee was meeting the very next day. We looked at the pri-
ority countries and felt nothing. No name popped off
the page or sounded compelling when we heard it pronounced. There were no Bible verses I could mysteri-
ously open to that said, "Get thee to Africa." How were
we to find guidance?

As we sat in the last row of our grammar theory class,
the August afternoon grew hot, as did the room. Drowsi-
ness dulled my concentration and I fought to stay awake.

We should never have sat in the back row, I thought as
I assessed my ability to understand and enjoy the depth
and breadth of linguistic theory. My imagination was
stirred as I fiddled with my pencil. I laid it down and
gave it a spin.

Hey, that works. I'll try it again.

I am not sure why, but I wrote in tiny letters the names
of all the countries Neil and I had been considering for
assignment. I arranged them neatly to fit on points of

the circumference of a small circle. Trying not to draw attention, I gave the pencil another spin, took note of the results and did it again.

Hmm. Same country.

By this time Neil was watching my game. He frowned. I wrote a note to him: "Two times so far on New Guinea."

He jotted back to me, "Three out of five."

I spun three more times.

"Three out of five on New Guinea," I scribbled.

Once again he returned my note: "Change the location of New Guinea."

I did, spun some more and reported the results: "Seven out of ten on New Guinea."

Others in the back row had noticed what I was doing. I showed them the note. There were raised eyebrows and scolding looks all around.

Hey, I'm not taking this seriously, I thought, shrugging my shoulders apologetically. *I'm just trying to stay awake!*

Later, back in the dorm room, I thought about it. The Lord could guide that way if He chose. I mean, seven out of ten, and I had changed the names around several times. Now I prayed, "Lord, we haven't seen any handwriting on the wall. Why *shouldn't* we go to New Guinea?"

We had seen several slide presentations during our two summers of training, and the two featuring the Territory of Papua and New Guinea had been particularly alluring. Not only was this South Pacific island, just north of Australia, beautiful, but hundreds of languages were spoken there in which not one verse of the Bible had ever been translated.

I had one more trick up my sleeve: to turn to the first verse I saw, upon opening the Bible, and see if it offered any help. Couldn't hurt. I opened to Proverbs and read the first verse I noticed, 16:33: "The lot is cast into the lap, but its every decision is from the LORD." I was shocked that what I was seeing actually made sense! Was this guidance?

Neil was not quite so impressed, but he did follow my reasoning that if we chose New Guinea, the Lord could certainly stop us if we had made a mistake. We had been praying all summer about where we should go, and so far we had no other leading.

The next day we told the committee our decision to go to the Territory of Papua and New Guinea. When we told our classmates, I could read the surprise in their faces—and doubt of our sanity. But I rather enjoyed the teasing about finding a new way to know the will of God.

What was it the Lord wanted me to learn from this? Could He have been saying that He would give guidance even when it comes in unusual forms? Despite my doubts about the deviant method by which we found direction, I felt a surprising peace about the decision.

Fourth Memorial Church in Spokane, the church I had attended since my conversion, seemed to enjoy sending us off to New Guinea. They made a fuss about our being "home-grown" missionaries. Within a short period of the church's history, they had sent out eight such missionaries, most of whom had been at that summer camp when I was thirteen—a record number of young people at the church from one generation to seek foreign service.

We felt like spoiled children with two hundred grandparents doting on our every whim. Everyone wanted to make sure we had our support quota met, our equipment ready to ship and our closets well supplied. Coming on the tail of the affirmation we had received during training, this treatment made the view from our mountaintop spectacular. We had to be God's gift to the South Pacific.

On March 1, 1972, we bid a sad but happy farewell to scores of family members and friends amid the flash of cameras, passing of hankies, hugs and handshakes. Not until I sat down in my airplane seat did the reality of actually saying goodbye hit me. This was the big moment we had anticipated for many years. I fought back the tears as we buckled our seatbelts.

"What? You're arriving on the fifth of March? I'm sorry, Neil, but we don't have any empty houses. You can't come to Ukarumpa. Are you sure you advised our office of your travel plans? We don't seem to have a record of it."

Neil was relaying the phone message back to me as I stood in the airport in Sydney, Australia, and told me he could not believe his ears.

We had just spent a couple of days visiting my only living Australian relative. If I had thought Mexico would be my only experience of culture shock, I had been dead wrong. The only difference was, this time I knew I was having culture shock. But that knowledge did not seem to relieve the stress.

I was anxious to leave this country where I had thought I would feel at home, but instead found myself making all kinds of silly mistakes. Diapers were nappies, cookies were biscuits, and there was no American mustard to put on my hamburger. Why hadn't my Australian mother warned me?

"We can go up to New Guinea," said Neil, "but we'll have to stay in Lae for a few days until they have a house for us."

"Lae? What will we do there?" I asked, picturing a small jungle outpost in my mind.

"The lady said we could stay in the guest house and do some shopping. Sounds like fun."

Neil could see an opportunity in any development.

Lae was beautiful. Lae was hot! This was my first taste of real tropical weather. I was assured by the other visitors at the missionary guest house that Ukarumpa, the SIL center located in the highlands some hundred miles to the northwest, was much cooler. While it lasted, though, it was pleasant to soak up the calls of exotic birds as I lounged comfortably under the palms.

Some other guests had the same idea, and soon I was joined by two women. We introduced ourselves and shared the usual small talk. Eventually the conversation was dominated by my two new acquaintances.

"I don't know if I can face going back to the village one more time. It's been so oppressive lately. I just have the feeling there is evil everywhere."

I listened with interest.

"I know what you mean. I'm struggling, too. I don't know why it's been so hard for me to learn the language, but I'm about ready to give up."

I sat in disbelief. How could these women talk like this? I had never heard a missionary discuss unresolved issues. There were always happy endings. But these women were in the middle of a battle, and it sounded as though they were losing.

Having survived six weeks of village living in Jungle Camp, I thought I knew all the answers. *It can't be that hard,* I thought to myself. *They must have done something wrong.*

I vowed to myself that it would never happen to me, no matter what. No, I would work very hard to avoid this kind of pitfall.

Managing to hold my doubts and fears at bay, I resolved in my mind over and over, *This will never happen to me.*

Into the Valley of the Shadow of Death

> To you I call, O LORD my Rock; do not turn a deaf ear to me. For if you remain silent, I will be like those who have gone down to the pit.
>
> Psalm 28:1

Dripping with perspiration, we stood in the coastal heat of the Lae airport while our pilot looked over the baggage. It was mid-March and we were finally embarking on the last leg of our journey. Despite the lingering jet lag, we were nervous with excitement.

"I can take only fifty kilos of baggage this trip," said the pilot. "The rest will come up later in the week. Can you pick out which cases have the items you need the most, and we'll load them onto the plane?"

He said this so casually that I assumed it was common practice. Hastily I chose a few suitcases, all the while trying to look calm and pleasant. First no house for us, then no baggage. What would the next surprise be?

As the Cessna 206 finally taxied into the Aiyura hangar at midday, I expected at least a brass band, perhaps the director for translation teams rushing out to meet the plane, exclaiming, "At last you've come!" But there were only aviation personnel going about their business and the wife of another passenger greeting him. As if this sort of thing happened every day!

Well, come to think of it, new translators probably did arrive frequently.

The pilot showed Neil and me the way to the aviation department vehicle that would carry us and our few meager suitcases to Ukarumpa, the main SIL center. He drove us about three kilometers down a bumpy dirt road before pulling up in front of our temporary new home—

What? The missionary guest house?

"Hello, I'm Nancy, the center hostess," the gracious woman said as she came out to meet us. "I'm really sorry about the housing situation but, as we said, we didn't know you were coming and we're fully occupied at the moment. But we did find a house you can stay in. Some ladies are over there now—er, ah, getting it ready for you. You can move in within the week," she added with a big smile.

As we walked into the guest house, a large, grand-motherly woman exclaimed, "Welcome to Ukarumpa! Will you need a cot for the little fellow?"

Oh, no, I thought, *an Australian. I'm doomed.*

Quick, why was she offering me a cot, of all things? I immediately pictured a foldout camping bed.

"Oh, no, thanks," I replied. "He'd fall out, don't you think?"

"Well, it's up to you, but if you change your mind, let me know. Your room is right there at the end of the passage."

I figured out all by myself that she meant the hallway. Heading for the room, I paused to look up. Strange, someone had tied a crib up in the open beam ceiling. I could use that.

"Excuse me, but this crib up here would be nice for my son. Do you suppose someone could get it down?"

"I asked you if you wanted a cot and you said no," she said, kind but puzzled. "I'll have someone get it down right away."

I had done it again. Was there no end? Cots, bickies, nappies—all these words I had never heard before. The business of just getting to where we wanted to be was proving to be more complicated and irritating than I had imagined. Was I doomed to be a linguistic failure? How come I could never figure out these things myself?

As Nancy had promised, we were soon in our house. It turned out that the family who owned the home had left Ukarumpa in a hurry because of a medical emergency. They had not had time to pack all their personal belongings so the house could be used for someone else. As it was the only place available for us, some volunteers had come in to pack for them.

I looked around the sparse quarters, dismayed that it did not look much like home. There were some basic items missing like mattresses, lamps and a washing machine.

"We'll just plug in the refrigerator, give you your matches to light the gas stove and you're in business," Nancy instructed us cheerily. "The ladies have left some group equipment for you—dishes and such. Let me know if there's anything I can do." And off she went on her never-ending rounds.

There were quite a few things I would need, and I panicked, remembering it would be some months before our crates arrived from the U.S.

"Looks like the first stop is the store," I said.

Neil, Heather, Danny and I headed out to walk the four blocks to a small building that housed the SIL center store. To my surprise it was fully stocked with all the necessities of life—even ice cream. I never dreamed there would be such a commodity in what certain books

I had read called a Stone Age country. We could not resist the temptation and added a half-gallon to our shopping cart.

Arriving home, we opened the refrigerator to put away the perishables. It was room temperature inside and, after a short inspection, found to be dead. Neil and I took out our list and added *refrigerator* to the other items we needed. Then, looking at one another in mock resignation, the four of us ate the whole half-gallon of ice cream on the spot.

Neil's first job at Ukarumpa, after he had spent almost two years studying linguistics and jungle training, was in the plumbing department. Danny started preschool and Heather was just old enough to enter kindergarten, so I was free to be assigned as a layout artist in the printing department. For three hours each morning I enjoyed drawing pictures for literacy books and helping with the layouts for the missionaries' printed newsletters.

Aside from washing diapers by hand, accidentally locking myself out of the house and finding that my K Mart sandals were not holding up in the New Guinea mud, life was tolerable.

April was a sad time for Ukarumpa. Despite an exceptional safety record, the twin-engine airplane flown by SIL, a Piper Aztec, crashed, killing seven people. Two of that number were nationals; five were members of Wycliffe/SIL. One was to have been our next-door neighbor.

Then an older man who had come as a short-term electrician suddenly slumped over and died of heart failure.

It was a time of mourning when people asked the question that was on our minds as well: What next?

Although our assignment was working at the center, we spent our spare time looking for the language group of our dreams. As I had never had any dreams about language groups, I found the task difficult. Neil, on the other hand, knew exactly what he wanted—a place where no missionary had gone before, "the ends of the earth."

We visited the language group that was then without a translator because of the plane crash deaths of those assigned there. No, that wasn't it. Too civilized.

We pored over maps and lists describing people groups of all kinds. Just reading forms and papers was not very inspiring.

Then it happened. Karl and Joice Franklin invited us for dinner and showed slides of Karl's latest survey trip. They had outlined an area within which the Folopa-speaking people (pronounced FO-do-pa) lived. I had not seen Neil so excited since the day he had read the literature about Bible translation for the first time. The next day he was on the phone making arrangements for a helicopter survey trip to visit this isolated group of people. I was not feeling too good, but decided I could not miss the trip. I had a sense this was going to be the one.

Staring intently from the helicopter down into the jungle, I was fascinated by the variety of canopied trees, flowering vines and colorful birds. Ken, the pilot, who had been over this ground on the recent linguistic survey, flew the helicopter low as we approached the first Folopa village.

Suddenly we were a thousand feet farther from the ground. I caught my breath as the ground dropped away beneath us and we flew over what Ken said was the Tua Gorge. We left jagged limestone cliffs behind us, but I looked ahead to see more cliffs on the other side. Then, glancing up, I saw Ken smiling as he enjoyed our surprise.

No sooner had we passed the gorge than I got my first glimpse of the unique *karst* formations. The "peaks," as they were called on the map, rose up sharply from the valley floor. *Peaks* hardly described the bizarre, dramatic shapes that now filled my vision. They looked more like teeth.

"You like this kind of stuff?" Ken asked Neil, who was grinning broadly and nodding his head in the affirmative. "You're a bushman true."

Glancing over at me, Ken shook his head from side to side as if to say, "I can't believe this guy."

We landed in four or five villages, attempting to interview anyone who could understand some Pidgin. In the village labeled by the mapmakers as Pupitao, we stopped to eat lunch in an old, empty building. (Later we learned it was the village church that had been started by a national evangelist a few years before our arrival.) No one seemed to understand English or Pidgin, but we were touched as we looked at the group of eager faces.

After we tried to explain that we wanted to translate the Bible into their language, one young man responded by stepping forward and saying in what I was sure were the only English words he could muster, "You come back!" His words rang in the air with warmth and sincerity.

Later, as Neil and I compared notes, we found we were both moved, especially by the surprise invitation. God, we felt, was calling us to this place. Why? Nothing about the location suggested any kind of comfort or ease. We had looked into the faces of a needy people who had nothing and they knew it. Yet both of us had said to this man, "Yes, we will come back."

Later that week the joyous word spread around our little neighborhood at Ukarumpa that we were seriously considering asking the translation director for an assignment to work with the Folopa-speaking people.

A neighbor arrived at my door one day to hear the details and offer to pray for us in the difficult decision. The gesture was welcome, but I picked up a note of foreboding in her concern. She confided her own experience of grave physical and emotional strain during her many years in the bush helping her husband in the translation work.

What was it I picked up in her prayer? A voice of warning about the sorrows and difficulties that lay ahead?

Soon she was gone and I was aware once again of that familiar, gnawing doubt.

I'm not sure about anything, I thought. *If God let that happen to her, what will happen to me?*

Anger rose up almost immediately to drive away the fear. *I will not have the same problems she did,* I cried to myself. In anguish I grabbed my Bible, opening to search for some word of comfort and guidance. To my astonishment I read these words:

> "You will go out in joy
>   and be led forth in peace;
> the mountains and hills
>   will burst into song before you,
> and all the trees of the field
>   will clap their hands."
>
> Isaiah 55:12

Immediately the fear evaporated as I realized that God was promising to take a hostile environment and provide a way for Neil and me to live and work there. How could we go wrong?

Another passage on the same page caught my attention:

> "As the rain and the snow
>   come down from heaven,
> and do not return to it
>   without watering the earth
> and making it bud and flourish,
>   so that it yields seed for the sower and bread for the
>   eater,
> so is my word that goes out from my mouth:
>   It will not return to me empty,
> but will accomplish what I desire
>   and achieve the purpose for which I sent it."
>
> Isaiah 55:10–11

God was going to use His Word to change lives—of that I was certain. The Folopa language was the place of God's appointment. I knew this was where we were to go.

The month of May was a very long month. I felt strange. Something was not right. Each day I felt weaker. I had scratched my finger on a diaper pin and noticed days later that it looked like a fresh cut.

The doctor at the center clinic was unable to diagnose anything with so little to go on.

A few days later an unimpressively small but red pimple in the center of each of my underarms was starting. Antibiotics were prescribed for the obvious infection, but after several more days I knew the treatment was not helping. The pain was increasing. After a while I could not sleep at night. Sores developed in my mouth, making it difficult for me to swallow. Stronger antibiotics and pain medications were given. These, too, seemed ineffective.

"Hi, my name is Lois. I live down the street. I heard Carol was sick." Lois Vincent stepped into the living room and surveyed the situation quickly.

Too sick to get up, I overheard the conversation from the tiny bedroom.

"You just go ahead with what you were doing," she told Neil. "I'll be in the kitchen washing up."

She bustled away and began ministering to the chaotic household.

The doctor who had been treating me had to leave the center because of another commitment. Other than the severe pain, the symptoms did not seem to indicate any extreme illness.

Lord, why are You doing this to me? I prayed frantically as the symptoms continued to worsen. *Am I going to die or what?*

In that dark hour, as I prayed, I heard the faint whisper of an answer in my head: *You will be healed.* It had to be God speaking. But I could not eat or sleep because of the pain. People we did not know came to pray with me for God's healing.

What's going on? I wondered as I continued to battle fear and the outlandish thought that God was either mistaken or He was betraying me.

The next day my neighbor Lois arrived to take her post. Neil described to her what kind of night we had just experienced. He was extremely worried after I had fainted on the way to the bathroom.

Lois could stand it no more. Although there was no official doctor on duty that day, she knew of a medically trained person who might possibly be available. David Lithgow had been a medical doctor years before becoming a Bible translator. Lois reached him on the telephone and asked him to come to our home.

David Lithgow, a tall, lanky fellow, was calm and quiet as he examined my underarms, looked into my mouth and listened to the latest developments in my illness. He never changed his expression as he observed that my armpits were in the process of turning black with gangrene. Quietly he went to the telephone and phoned the aviation department.

"We need a 206 immediately for a medical evacuation." Pause. "No planes? No, a helicopter won't do. She has to lie down. You sure there's nothing available? All right."

David calmly wrote a letter of his findings to the doctor at the hospital who would receive me. "Guess you'll have to go by road, but you'd better drive as fast as you can."

Go by road? We didn't even have a car.

Just then another neighbor knocked at the door.

"Say, how's your wife?" Vic asked Neil as he entered and heard the news. "I have a car. I had the strangest dream last night." And he went on to share the dream, which was complicated and symbolic.

"I think the Lord was telling me that I'm supposed to drive you to the hospital," he concluded.

We were not sure how it all fit but were willing to trust his judgment.

Lois took the children, Neil closed up the house and the nightmare experience continued.

Miles and miles of staring at blue sky from the back of a station wagon. I could not sit up to see where we were going. All I knew were the endless bumps of a gravel road.

Hospital, that's the place where they make people well. If I can only get to the hospital, I'll get better.

It was only sixty miles to Goroka, the small Eastern Highlands town where the government hospital was located. But the trip seemed to take hours.

Concerned faces surrounded me and my confidence surged.

Move to the stretcher. Careful, don't drop me now. That's it.

Why were these crazy thoughts going through my head?

Lying in the hospital room, I enjoyed the fact that everyone was running around suddenly, getting on my case.

A nurse was asking me for information. *How old am I? Can't remember.*

"Twenty-five," I replied.

Wait, didn't I just have a birthday a couple of weeks ago? I'm 26.

Too late; she had left the room.

I'll just take a little nap until she gets back.

"Mr. Anderson, your wife is very sick," the doctor confided to Neil. "She may not make it—that's how sick she is. The next 24 hours will be decisive. We'll do everything we can."

I never got to hear those words. I had already left the scene, deep in a coma.

I Don't Get It, Lord

> "Will the Lord reject forever? Will he never show his favor again? Has his unfailing love vanished forever? Has his promise failed for all time? Has God forgotten to be merciful? Has he in anger withheld his compassion?"
>
> Psalm 77:7–9

eil, we'll have to send them back," I raved.

"Send who back?"

"Those children. We don't have enough shoes for five children."

"Carol, we don't have five children."

"Yes, we do. You've forgotten, that's all. Remember, they were drowning."

"Wait a minute."

Neil opened the hospital room door, leaned out and searched the hallway. Noreen, a fellow Wycliffe member, was standing beside the nursing station waiting to receive word on her daughter, who had fallen out of a tree and received a concussion.

"Noreen, can you come in here for a minute? Will you tell Carol how many children we have? She just woke up from the coma and thinks we have five children."

"Carol, you have two children," Noreen said sweetly.

What? The mental haze was clearing and suddenly I knew it was true. It had been a dream, but it had seemed so real. That whole week I had gone in and out of bizarre, vivid dreams, Technicolor mind productions. I dreamed that I could will myself from the room by jumping out the window when no one was looking. A 747 jumbo jet had landed just outside the hospital and all our friends from home came to visit me. The week wound up with my rescuing three drowning children and adopting them.

Now it was Saturday morning. I had come to the hospital on Monday. I tried to focus my vision and look around the room. Everyone was grinning.

What's the joke? I missed it, I thought as I tried to move and found little response from my body. It was hard to talk. I felt that I was enunciating perfectly, but when I spoke, everyone looked at me as though I were talking gibberish. Neil gave me a piece of paper and a pen.

"Here, see if you can write it," he said. "Maybe I'll understand that."

I wrote slowly and painstakingly.

Neil stared in disbelief and chuckled. "I can't make out any words from this!"

Gradually I awoke and started to speak more clearly. I had the distinct impression that I had come to in the middle of some drama. What had taken place during those days I had been comatose that left everyone in such a good humor?

A young Australian man in a white hospital coat was showing Neil a piece of paper. "Look at this!" he said excitedly. "The white cell count was down to five hundred until Thursday morning. But when we tested the count this morning, it had risen dramatically. This is unheard of! I had to come see for myself."

The technician laid out the slides he had prepared during the week to illustrate his amazement.

The cause of my illness was determined to be a reaction to the medication we all took weekly to prevent malaria. This kind of reaction was rare but fatal in almost one hundred percent of the cases observed. The drug had shocked my bone marrow into a paralysis that meant it would no longer produce white corpuscles, and there was no known treatment to stimulate renewed production.

So what had happened on Thursday?

In Dreamland I was riding in a black car down a beautiful, wooded country lane. My traveling companions were bearded men dressed in black suits and old-fashioned top hats. Slowly, almost reverently we motored down the lane until reaching a small church nestled in the forest. After parking the car, we walked slowly into the quaint building, and I sat down on an old oak chair in the middle of the Sunday school room. The men in black gathered around me, laid their hands on my shoulders and began to pray.

This is a very serious occasion, I thought, trying to look somber and respectful. *I guess I am pretty sick, though.*

"Thank you for what you've done," I said to the men as they finished praying.

Then we returned in slow motion to the black car and drove away.

"Thank you for what you've done," I said as I lay in the hospital bed, eyes closed, as yet unresponsive to the outside world.

The men who had gathered to pray for me, dressed in white hospital gowns and masks, stared at one another in amazement. Had this critically sick woman heard them, in her comatose state, praying? Did she know what was going on in the room?

Two days would elapse before I came back to stay.

A putrid smell assailed my nostrils. At first I did not notice it, but it got worse the more alert I became.

A nurse appeared at my side looking businesslike but cheerful.

"Now let's just move your arms up here," she remarked as she attempted to raise my stiff limbs. "There, you shouldn't feel this, but just in case it hurts, let me know."

I had no idea what she was doing as she worked away on my left armpit. A gray pile began to build up in a kidney bowl at the edge of the bed. The nurse continued to chat about how the bad smell would be all gone soon. I finally put two and two together and realized that gray stuff was me, or used to be me. The horror of my discovery was overwhelming. I started to scream uncontrollably.

"Now, Mrs. Anderson, it shouldn't hurt. It's dead flesh. Stop that. I'm not hurting you."

I knew she was right. My body was not in pain. What I could not explain to her was the impact this was having on the rest of me. Everyone assumed when I awoke that I understood what was going on. But I did not begin to comprehend the extent of my illness or what had taken place in my body as a result. The doctor had mentioned something about the possibility of my losing my arms, but that piece of information had not lodged anywhere in my brain.

I heard a commotion in the hallway and suddenly realized that my protests were probably disturbing other patients. I imagined them stirring uncomfortably in their beds as they listened to this crazed woman across the corridor from them.

"What's happening to that poor woman?" a tearful patient asked the attendant on duty just outside my door.

"Oh, it's nothing to worry about," he replied. "Just someone who was very ill and has gangrene. She's not in pain, so there's absolutely nothing to be concerned about."

Clenching her teeth and apparently calling on every ounce of fortitude, the nurse in my room finally finished her job.

I had thought when I woke up that my suffering was over, but it was just beginning.

Neil and the others had agonized during my coma. While I was having an outer space vacation, they waited to see if I would live. Now, as get-well cards, letters of congratulations and even a poster signed with the message "Think of all the time you'll have to read your Bible and pray!" arrived from around the world, I stared blankly at my surroundings. I was being extolled for enduring this worst of all trials and being used by God to bless so many. I felt that people were smiling at me expectantly and waiting for me to return the happy sentiments. But instead of joy and thanksgiving, there was shock and disappointment. Reading my Bible was useless. My prayers fell with a thud onto the concrete floor. Why did I feel as if I had descended into hell?

Once the dead tissue had been removed from my underarms, there were gaping wounds of raw flesh that required daily dressing. The pain from the exposed nerves was not constant. It lasted only as long as it took them to change the bandages once a day.

This was not a pleasant task for the hospital staff either. A nurse named Heather lost her composure one day and her stern rebuke stuck in my mind: "Mrs. Anderson, it's only pain!"

It's only pain. I knew there must be deep meaning in there somewhere, but it would take quite a bit of thought before I settled on what the meaning was. Meanwhile, they were only tears I was crying. Nothing to worry about. It just felt as though someone were holding a flame under each arm for about an hour as the dressings were removed each day.

Goroka Hospital in the cool highlands passed me on after five weeks to the hospital in the coastal capital of the Territory of Papua and New Guinea called Port Moresby. I had healed enough so that the next seven weeks were cheerier. Because they put me into a room with six beds, I had a constant variety of roommates. The hospital ward itself was outdoorsy. The building was a long, narrow line of rooms with a covered verandah corridor. The heat necessitated ceiling fans and a whole wall of louvered windows to let the breeze blow through.

In order to help me get my strength back, Neil was encouraged by the staff to take me for walks. We could also sit outside on park benches and enjoy the beautiful tropical days.

Shortly after I was transferred to Port Moresby, a nurse commented, "I suppose you hate this country now. I'll bet you just want to pack right up and go home, after what you've been through."

"No," I replied, "I'm staying."

Although I could easily contradict this nurse, her question made me think. I had been through a lot but I did not want to quit. This was God's plan for our lives. We were called to be missionaries and do the work of Bible translation.

There were other uncomfortable, nagging questions, however, that I did not want to think about. *Why did God let this happen? Have I done something wrong? Is the Lord displeased with me?*

As I continued to recuperate, Neil spent some of his time inquiring about the mission that operated in the area inhabited by the Folopa people. He was pleased to find out that it sponsored a church in Port Moresby attended by these missionaries. So the very first Sunday after I was transferred, he visited the Evangelical Church of Papua, a church that grew out of the work of Asia Pacific Christian Mission.

"You'll never guess!" he told me later. "I met a whole group of Folopa-speaking people at the ΛPCM church. A man named Mosa agreed to come three times a week to the hospital and teach us the language through the medium of Melanesian Pidgin."

I was amazed at this turn of events. Although countless people around the globe had somehow benefited from my illness, this seemed to be the first positive result for us.

"Yu tok wanem? 'Dispela em wanem samting'?"

As the three of us sat on an outdoor bench at the Port Moresby hospital, Neil was asking Mosa how to say, "What is this?" in Folopa—a handy phrase to have at one's disposal when entering an unknown language.

"Ee no aye?" came the reply from Mosa, and our pencils scribbled in our notebooks just the way we had learned in our training.

What a thrill as I heard these first words in Folopa! I savored the sound as I thought, *This is our very own language. We have begun our work and my ordeal is truly behind me.*

The hours went much faster now that I had something to do besides receive whopping shots of antibiotics and have trips to the operating room for more skin grafts. I was also pretty sick of the physical therapy woman, who seemed determined to twist off my frozen arm joints.

After three torturous months, they released me from the hospital, and Neil and I were on our way back to our two children and the future.

Once our family life was restored and we made plans to begin our work in the Folopa language, things went smoothly. Neil and Alex Vincent (the husband of our helpful neighbor Lois) undertook a ten-day survey trip led by Mosa. Neil told me later they trudged up and down ridges while being bitten by mosquitoes, leeches and various six-legged creatures. Mosa acted as interpreter while Neil explained to a succession of villages that he and his wife were willing to come and translate parts of the Bible into their language and teach them to read. And to the village that responded with the most enthusiasm would go the opportunity to have us for neighbors for the next fifteen to twenty years.

All the responses were positive but no one showed more excitement than the people at Fukutao (the one the map had called Pupitao), who had urged us many months before to come back. Since this village was located in the center of the language area, it seemed the best place to begin work.

Neil left for a month, this time building our house in Fukutao village. My evenings were pretty quiet in our little rented home after the children were in bed. The place still looked stark and empty, even though our crates from home had arrived and we had unpacked our things.

The evening was chilly at five thousand feet elevation, even though the equator was not far to the north. I put on a sweater and looked around the little bedroom. What to do? Entertainment had been far from our thinking when we packed to come to this country. Once the activity ceased, the talking stopped and the quiet set in, I had little to do but think.

O God, what will happen if I stop and think?

My thoughts were making me uneasy. Once again I found them returning to the months of illness and hospitalization that I had been trying to forget. Many people had been interested in my recovery, although I could scarcely understand why. The mail had come from people all over the world telling me what a joyful experience my illness had been for them. All-night prayer meetings had been held, at Ukarumpa and at our home church in Spokane, in which revival had taken place. A wonderful result, I knew. So why was I finding myself so angered by it?

I had been the one to suffer while they got the blessings.

I remembered the poster with the message "Think of all the time you'll have to read your Bible and pray!" How many times *had* I tried to read my Bible and pray, only to feel the same emptiness I was feeling now? Why?

I must do something, I thought as I sat in my bedroom. *It's too quiet.*

I picked up a book someone had given me, trying vainly to divert my thoughts. As I opened to the middle and plunged in blindly, my eyes fell on these words: "But it is healthy to hate one's soul."

Healthy to hate one's soul? This was not much context with which to judge a book, but I quickly lost interest in it. The effect of that one phrase felt like a kick in the stomach. In that moment I was aware of intense pain and anger that had, no doubt, been simmering for months. I had worked hard at not allowing them to surface. But the phrase from the book triggered a release of my darkest suspicions—it was God who hated my soul. He was the One who had let me suffer. I must have missed the way somewhere for Him to have let this happen.

Was I actually angry with God? I wanted to answer, *Of course not!* But I couldn't. I threw my fist up to heaven and exclaimed, "I don't hate my life, I love it! It's my life, mind, soul and spirit! How dare You tamper with them?"

Then it flashed before me that I had spent all those months, both in the hospital and afterward, trying to pretend I was on top of the whole experience. Oh, it was true that God had miraculously healed me of a terminal illness. My life had been spared and I had been restored to near-perfect health. There was much to be thankful for.

But I really had suffered. And I had undergone more than physical pain there in the hospital, although no one had seen it. I had endured terrible temptations to believe that God had abandoned me in my hour of need. I believed He had promised to heal me, and I assumed that the healing would mean deliverance from further suffering. But it had not happened that way and I could not understand why. God was supposed to be my heavenly Father! I had thought He would protect me since I was here to do His work. Did He even care that I had suffered?

On my knees in the darkened little bedroom, I poured out my anger.

"God, I am so mad at You! I didn't deserve this. Didn't I give my life to be a missionary? Didn't I have my devotions every day? I'm not a bad person. So why are You punishing me?"

Even as I asked these questions, my anger dissolved in the loving presence of my Father. I knew in a moment that He accepted my outburst, that He was glad I had been honest. And I saw all too clearly the foolishness of being angry with a sovereign God. Was I actually accusing Him of not loving me?

It all happened quickly—confession, relief. No logical reasoning produced these emotions; they were the result of the Lord's healing touch on my wounded spirit.

"Lord, I know Your Word says You are good," I continued. "Forgive me for being angry with You and for not believing that You know what You're doing. But I just don't understand why this happened to me."

Even as I prayed, His warm presence glowed, much as it had on the top bunk in a camp cabin many years before. I felt the freedom to continue.

"There's just one question. Why did this happen to me? Why did I have to suffer?"

I did not expect an answer. Merely asking the question released something that had been blocked up and hurting for a long time.

As if whispered inside a warm cloud, an answer came. It was very clear in my mind.

Because I love you.

This was not what I expected. For a few moments I knelt at the dark bedside in stunned silence. Of course God loved me. I knew that. But when I asked Him why I had to suffer. . . .

What could this mean? I guessed it meant that was all I needed to know just then.

There in the dark, the closeness I sensed with the Lord began to fade, and I found myself once again in a cold room.

The encounter left me awestruck. What kind of God was this? He had sent me to a foreign land to do His work, promising to protect and care for me. Then I had run into one problem after another, finally almost losing my life.

I had realized, of course, that there would be some trials and suffering in my missionary career. But maybe I had expected only a little persecution for my faith. I certainly had not anticipated physical pain and near-death.

The pain and struggle had been overshadowed by the presence of God. What He had said to me was enough, but I found myself still brooding and confused.

I just did not get it.

For Better or Worse

If the LORD delights in a man's way, he makes his steps firm; though he stumble, he will not fall, for the LORD upholds him with his hand.

Psalm 37:23–24

"Come on in and have a seat." Harry Wiemer, the director for translation teams, motioned Neil and me toward the two wooden office chairs. Harry was a man with many years of learning from his own trials as a Bible translator.

After the exchange of greetings and small talk, he looked at us both with a serious face. "I assume you know what you're getting into, don't you? The Folopa people live in a very isolated part of the country. You'll be the first team to locate in a remote region because of the availability of the helicopter."

We had become aware that helicopters were not normally used for missionary transportation. Only in the last year had an experimental program been started to see if such a thing was feasible. We would be a test case.

"If it breaks down," he said, "have you thought that you may have to walk three days to get out?" He looked carefully for our reactions.

"Yes," Neil said with a smile and more than a hint of glee.

"This is a long-term commitment," Harry continued, "so you want to be sure you're both happy about this decision." He turned to look directly at me, searching for any signs of misgiving. "Carol, what do you think of all this? Is this your wish as well?"

I could not imagine, with the vision in my mind's eye of a young man beckoning to us, saying, "You come back," how I would ever change my mind.

"Yes," I responded. "This is where I want to go."

"Are you fully recovered from your illness and strong enough to stand up to the rigors of living in the bush for months at a time?" Perhaps he was unable to believe that one who was so close to death and who had spent three months in the hospital recuperating could now be sitting before him asking to be sent to this Siberia-like location.

We would be spending several months at a time in the village before taking breaks to attend workshops and catch up with other tasks associated with our assignment. We all knew this would be very demanding physically, emotionally and spiritually, even if it were not in such a faraway location.

"Yes," I reassured him. "I believe I've fully recovered."

"Well, then, you have my blessing." He added, with a look of wisdom and patience, just in case the idea had not crossed our minds, "This could be a very tough place to work."

But untested idealism was soaring high at that moment. I thought, *We can do this.*

The interview was over and Neil and I had just said, "I do." Now we were committed, for better or worse, for as long as it would take to finish the translation.

The honeymoon was short.

"Your cargo is overweight."

The aviation coordinator could hardly believe his eyes
as he surveyed the boxes I presented to him the morning of our official allocation flight to Fukutao village.
Having given no thought to the limitations of the aircraft, I had bought enough food to stock a small army
for our first three-month stay. By the time our personal
items and building supplies were added in, we were
hopelessly beyond the limit of the combination of the
helicopter and the Cessna 206.

"You'll have to knock off a hundred kilos," he said
apologetically, looking over all the gear. "What's in these
boxes, Carol?"

I stood there too numb to answer, let alone think. I
had not written the contents on the outsides before they
were tied securely with twine. Finally I said tentatively,
"I think this one is the school supplies."

"Maybe you can do without the cases of food. The village people will probably sell you sweet potato."

He was being helpful but I gulped at the thought. No
flour, no sugar?

After half an hour of putting boxes back into the
hangar for storage, the loading was completed and we
were on our way, with the boxes in the airplane and the
kids and me in the helicopter. We were joining Neil, who
had been in Fukutao for the last several weeks continuing to work on our house.

Flying over the countryside that morning, I pressed my
face up against the bubble window as I tried not to miss
anything interesting. The highlands had their share of
forest and mountains, but small gardens and villages dot-
ted the surface below with surprising frequency. Much of
the landscape was covered with tall, wavy kunai grass.

Forty minutes into the flight, the terrain began to
change. Gone were the neat gardens and clearings with
tidy arrangements of round and rectangular houses.
Now I saw only jagged mountains; long, sharp ridges
running east to west; and the strange eruptions of for-
est-covered earth and rock that Neil and I had observed

the last time we were here. The formations reminded me of a severe case of land acne, poorly disguised by the heavy forest covering. I could see a twisted, brown ribbon of water running in crazy loops and turns as we neared our destination. How true the travel poster that claimed, "Like every place you've never been."

A whole year had passed since our arrival in the territory. We had done our best to prepare for any and all situations. There was much to learn.

The 2,500 speakers of Folopa were scattered in seventeen groupings of hamlets in an area that stretched over one hundred square miles of rain forest. Fukutao village was one of the largest groups, with a population of some three hundred people divided into twelve different clans, or extended families.

Life was simple for them and involved mostly trying to stay alive. Hunting for game like wild pigs, cassowary birds, possums and pythons was a favorite with the men. For the everyday variety of vegetables and fruits, like sweet potato, yams, taro, squash, bananas, pineapple and papaya, gardens were hacked out of steep mountainside underbrush.

Women maintained and harvested the gardens, which meant lots of heavy carrying up and down very rough terrain.

In our first days of village life, we saw how our new neighbors carried out their daily routines. It went like this: Up with hungry babies at the crack of dawn, feed the family, feed the domesticated pigs, soak up the little bit of sunshine for the day, gossip with the neighbors while weaving a bark string carrying bag, then head off to the garden. Arrive home just before dark, in time to feed the kids again, wrap the aching bodies in beaten bark cloth capes, go to sleep and start the whole thing again the next day.

Inside our house I was running back and forth from the kitchen table helping Heather, age six, with her kindergarten lessons, to the front porch writing down Folopa words, back into the house to sweep mud from the floors and spider webs from the roof, back to the front porch, and down to the other end of the house to encourage Danny, almost three, to play with the village children. When someone asked, "Where are my socks?" I would spend a half-hour rummaging through boxes and piles. With that and cooking meals, my days were full.

Neil, meanwhile, carried on the task of finishing the house. This included an upstairs workshop for his never-ending fix-it jobs, and a separate building for language work and Bible translation that the Folopa people called the Bible house. For the time that we would begin a literacy teaching program in the village, we had plans to build another structure to house that project. But for the beginning stages, our home and study building were sufficient.

Learning the language, I thought, would be easy. After all, I had taken three years of Spanish in high school and that was not so bad. Also, Neil and I were counting heavily on the pages of notes taken from conversations with Mosa in Port Moresby. With this boost, how could we go wrong?

"*Hịka wisi,*" I ventured on one of those first mornings as I greeted the father of Hariso, the little girl about Danny's age, and the men who held up the doorposts. We had been assured by Mosa that the literal greeting *Good morning* was proper Folopa.

But the lack of any kind of reaction from the men told me what I had suspected for several days now. This was not a Folopa sort of thing to say. Well, what about the rest of the data?

"*Yaọo na dele?*" I was attempting to ask. ("Is that your dog?")

There was a mumbling sound as the men conferred quietly with one another. I repeated my question. Then one of the men stepped forward and tried to explain something.

I could not understand much but made out the words *Sipiso fo* in there somewhere. Could they mean Sopese, the name of Mosa's village? Why were they pronouncing it wrong? I listened further as they tried to tell me how to say "Is that your dog?" the *right* way.

The men wrinkled up their noses at the apparently distasteful sounds of the southern dialect and looked as if they would spit. The mispronunciation of the village name seemed to cap off their disgust. Perhaps the men of Sopese village had told the mapmakers to spell the name of our village *Pupitao*.

Just then Pastor Yonape walked toward us. I remembered that he was not from this village or language, even though he spoke it well.

"Pastor, can you help me?" I asked, speaking the more familiar Pidgin language. I repeated the phrase I had used and asked, "Is there something wrong with saying that?"

He confirmed my suspicions. "Heto Hama, the people in Fukutao village don't say it that way. That's the talk of Sopese village."

I was speaking the language all right. But the dialect was just different enough that it was not acceptable.

"What about the village two days' walk over to the east?" I asked.

"That's another talk," he replied, smiling, grateful for a chance to help me.

I thought about the seventeen villages and wondered if each had a different version of the Folopa language.

By asking, "What is it?" or by watching and listening to explanations of an event until something clicked, Neil and I slowly put pieces of the puzzle together. When I thought I had discovered something new, I wrote it down in my notebook. Neil, on the other hand, spent most of his time outside the house. He was working on projects to finish the building of our house, which required the help of other men. No matter what he was doing, he was talking all the time and almost never wrote things down on paper.

Sitting on the front porch one morning, I was determined to find out everyone's names. How was it that we had lived in the village for weeks and still did not know people's names?

"What's your name?" I asked a young girl who sat on my porch. She must have been about eight years old, even though she was the same size as my six-year-old daughter, Heather, who sat with her.

The clothing all the children wore was very old and worn. Some shirts were just connected strings with the rest completely torn away.

"Nepiame," she replied, slowly and carefully.

"My name is Kero." I had given up trying to get them to say *Carol*.

"Épó," she responded, which meant *yes*.

I wondered why she did not repeat my name after me. Then I pointed to an old woman huddled in her bark cape. This wraparound garment had started out as the inside layer of a wide strip of bark. It had been beaten with a club until it spread out and made a rough cloth. The top was gathered with bark string and reached almost to her feet, so that the enclosed figure almost disappeared within the brown cocoon. The traditional, all-purpose cape was a common sight in the morning air when the fog still hung close to the ground.

"Her name is—?"

Nepiame leaned over close to me and whispered a name in my ear. The old woman frowned and complained loudly. At this Nepiame shook her head and said a different word, aloud this time. Soon I realized this was the term for *grandmother*.

What had I said that offended this woman so that she turned her back on us and mumbled under her breath?

Nepiame looked at me apologetically. "Don't say her name. It's not good."

"What name do I say?" I asked. "Grandmother?"

"Fisini Hama," was the reply.

I was to call this older woman by her daughter's name, with the addition of *hama,* mother, on the end. I remembered meeting her daughter Fisini a few days earlier.

Now I said the name *Fisini Hama* and the old woman brightened considerably.

After this I began listening to people talking to each other outside my window. They called each other by kinship terms or by someone's *hama,* mother, or *ali,* father. I had been very impolite, I realized, in trying to ascertain everyone's names. On the other hand, I would not learn who anyone was unless I knew the names of their children, some of whom were also parents. This information would have to be extracted carefully and quietly, not as I had been doing.

A short time after this, Neil and I decided it was time to find out once and for all which children went with which families. It was confusing trying to piece the relationships together. Rather than wander around the village trying to place everyone, we decided to have each of the thirty families to our house for a meal.

After entertaining several families, we got into a routine. Our guests got to know for the most part what to expect. It was a learning experience for everyone, and none of us caught on quickly to the great differences in our two cultures. But each week the verbal invitation would go out and on Friday afternoons our ritual began.

Curious brown faces pressed against the window as the growing darkness outside made my little kitchen glow with light. I wondered if they were curious about what the "red" people were up to. Strange how we think of ourselves as white in contrast to their dark skin. No doubt the first Caucasian person they ever saw was beet-red from hiking up the mountainside to their village, and thus their reference.

The battery-powered bulb attracted moths, and one by one they swirled upward out of nowhere to begin their futile aerial dance.

Neil held the door open as a man in his late thirties stepped forward.

"*Koneo*, Naniae Ali," Neil greeted the visitor.

Naniae Ali (Naniae's father) crouched slightly from habit as he passed through what to him was a large door frame. Folopa houses required a bent posture, as their doors were shorter than the average adult. As he entered, leading a girl about ten years old, his face registered his amazement. The height of the roof, the flatness of the floor, the sight of bright light and the variety of furnishings transcended any previous experience.

Heather and Dan rushed from behind the curtained doorway that led into the back part of our house as soon as they saw the familiar girl. Apprehension melted into smiles of joy as the children met in the center of the room. Soon they were communicating with nods and gestures, as children often do when language fails them.

Next a woman clad in a simple, gathered skirt and faded, loosely hanging blouse crept inside, as if a false move might disturb or damage the delicate surroundings. She removed her bark cape and a string bag that hung from the crown of her head. I had noticed that Folopa women, as well as most of the women in the country, were expert at making string from tiny strips of fiber and then weaving unique, stretchable bags for carrying. Naniae's mother was no exception. The bag that held her baby was made with a very wide opening so the child could be lifted in and out easily. Inside the bag a chubby, eight-month-old baby continued his comfortable sleep.

A boy of about sixteen grinned broadly as he marched past the threshold.

Following him was the last member of the family, a thin, gray-haired, older man. He grabbed Neil's hand warmly, shaking it up and down as he declared, "*Be wisi*" ("Good house") with a twinkle in his eye.

Neil showed the guests to the table, which was set with enameled metal plates and large spoons.

As the grandfather approached a bench, he seemed to recognize that it was for sitting, but he had probably never actually seen anyone do this. So he stood on it and squatted. A quick rebuke from his grandson and a demonstration of the correct position brought embarrassed smiles from the adults and giggles from the younger set.

There were introductions as we tried to get the children's names—Naniae, the son; Kepawhiso, the daughter; and baby Opereke. Now Neil and I knew better than to ask the adults their names, but we hoped during the course of the evening to find out who was related to whom.

I had prepared a kind of stew that I thought contained the best of both worlds—sweet potato, stew beef and powdered soup mix. It never occurred to me that perhaps this mixture would not be very appealing to people who did not spice their food. Confidently I placed my creation in the center of the table next to the bread, which I knew everyone liked. There was also canned butter and a bowl of salt.

"Take some salt," I urged Naniae Ali during the course of the meal.

I motioned to him to help himself, knowing the Folopas loved salt.

He dipped his large spoon into the bowl until the salt was heaped up high, then passed it slowly to his mouth. The whole spoonful went in as Neil and I watched, horrified.

I decided against encouraging everyone to help themselves to the butter.

Neil dished out the stew carefully into the bowl-like plates, thanked the Lord for the food in his halting Folopa, and we started to eat.

At first it was quiet. I watched intently and listened to make sure everyone was comfortable with the proceedings. The men plunged right in, enthusiastically savoring each bite of the strange concoction. Naniae's mother, however, looked dejected at the prospect of eating unfamiliar food.

Neil and I began to ask questions as best we could, and soon the conversation relaxed. I struggled and strained to understand our guests' answers and come up with intelligent-sounding responses.

"There's an older son, Sei, but he's away hunting," Naniae's father said, glancing at Naniae, the sixteen-year-old.

He held his hand up to show outstretched fingers. Pressing the small finger to his palm, he thrust his hand out and said the name *Sei*. He looked toward Naniae and pressed the ring finger into his palm, indicating that he was the second child. The middle finger now joined the other two as he tilted his head to the side in a pathetic expression and said mournfully, *"Senaane kisine sukanepó."* ("A girl died of sickness.") Pointing his chin in the direction of the next child, the younger girl, Kepawhiso, four fingers curled into a partial fist, leaving only the thumb. Finally he bent his thumb under the other fingers to signify five children born to him—the last, of course, being the infant, Opereke.

I kept repeating the names so I would not forget.

"Last week my brother came and ate food."

Let's see, that would have been Owarape's father, the head man.

"Your father . . . house . . . there?" I tried to ask.

The mother smiled and supplied the missing words as I sorted out her family members.

The baby began to stir. He was lifted from his tiny string-and-bark bed. The net bag was removed from her lap, the blouse was lifted and a breast was steered into the searching mouth.

The male members of the family had all finished their first helping and looked eagerly toward the big pot in the center of the table. Pushing bits of meat to one side of the dish and bits of sweet potato to the other, Naniae's mother and sister looked as yet uncertain about eating the stew.

My curiosity got the better of me. "The food, is it not good?"

"It's very good, but if I eat it I will throw up," came Naniae Hama's sheepish reply.

Poor woman, she's not feeling well.

"Koneo," I responded. ("I'm sorry.")

I was confused as she took another piece of bread, wolfing it down with globs of butter.

Seconds were eaten with all the gusto of the first round. They continued to eye the remaining food.

They can't still be hungry, I thought as I noticed a look of anxiety growing in their expressions.

Just then my attention was turned to the sounds coming from the other side of the wall. Outside the house people were talking but attempting to sound as if they were whispering. People were always outside our house, and they were always talking, so this was not unusual. But suddenly I realized some kind of communication was going on between those outside and our visitors inside.

Naniae's grandfather pushed back the bench and rose from the table. With no explanation he got down on his hands and knees near the base of the wall. The loud whispering continued. The family at the table made beating motions in the air to chastise their relative for his embarrassing behavior and try to get him to return to his place.

"Huh?" he grunted, trying to understand the muffled speech through the bark wall.

Neil and I looked at each other, wondering what was going on.

Then, without any warning, the old man got up, returned to the table and retrieved his plate full of food. He reached over to the serving bowl, heaped on one more scoop of stew and placed some bread alongside for good measure. Motioning to his grandson to open the window for him, he walked over to it and peered into the darkness. Through the open window a hand appeared, reach-

ing for the prize, and the meal was delivered. Muted
hoots and howls of delight could be heard.

"*Mo keeeee*, Heto Ali, Heto Hama!" ("Thank you,
Heather's father and mother.")

I gave in to my curiosity and opened the front door.
A group of ten or so people was huddled over the plate,
disbursing the food painstakingly to everyone amid
sounds of pleasure.

With mouth full but smiling, Naniae's cousin looked
up and said in his language, "Thank you! It's delicious!"

The eaters all agreed and repeated their appreciation.

As I closed the door, Neil and I looked at each other
once again, searching for answers. We had thought we
were inviting a family to dinner, but our definition of
family and theirs were apparently very different.

Once our guests intuited that we understood the concept of the larger family, metal plates appeared from a
string bag I had not noticed being brought in. We coop-
erated by emptying the leftovers into their containers.

The final touch to the evening came when we gave a
guided tour of our house. We had decided from the start
that it would not be wise to give the villagers free access
to our home while we were living there. The stress of
people walking in and out would have been too much
for our family. Instead we gave a tour so everyone could
see how we lived.

"*Haiyoo!*" exclaimed Naniae's mother as she flicked a
thumbnail on her front tooth and gave the characteris-
tic Folopa cluck. She was studying the bathroom faucet
out of which water flowed, caught from rain on the roof
and stored in a tank next to the house.

"*Haiyooo!*" she exclaimed even more loudly when she
caught sight of herself in the multi-tile mirror in the bedroom. Bending toward the glass, she reached up and
touched her face, as if she could not believe it was really
she.

The next wonder was our individual beds and bed-
rooms. The master bedroom was of utmost interest as
Neil explained that he and I slept in the same bed. This

was a frightening concept to people whose survival depended on spacing the birth of children far enough apart to improve their chances of living. As there was no birth control available, distance between married partners was the only responsible way to assure safety for the young. The Folopas would never sleep in the same quarters, opting for very occasional trysts in the privacy of a distant garden hideaway.

After the last room was examined and the tour ended, we sent our visitors on their way, the whole group laughing and talking loudly about their evening.

Once the dishes were washed and it was time to turn off the electrical generator, I was drained. Each time we had one of these encounters, we learned new things. This night had been no exception. Sometimes I marveled that I, who had read so many anthropology books, was still so ignorant when it came down to face-to-face cultural contacts. I tried hard to understand and respond in some adult-sounding way. But if it were not for the innate Folopa intelligence in linguistic deciphering, there would be no chance of communicating I was sure of that.

Back in the director's office when I had said, "I do," I had meant it. Like marriage, the job held many fantasies and wonderful expectations that I had entertained ahead of time. Problems came when false expectations did not die but lived on to produce guilt and shame. Somewhere someone was doing a better job at this than I was. Neil and I were still in the very early stages of the task, but I knew that some missionary wives had learned the language with incredible speed, or created and organized entire literacy programs in their places of assignment, or led Bible studies or even translated the Scriptures themselves.

At the moment my potential for the future was not looking very good. I just hoped God would not lose His patience with me.

All Spiders
Great and Small

How many are your works, O LORD! In wisdom
you made them all; the earth is full of your creatures.
Psalm 104:24

A young, innocent face looked up into mine. Baro smiled and held up his clenched fist toward my waiting jar. Suddenly I heard a bloodcurdling scream . . . and realized it was me.

Neil came running from somewhere and found me cowering in the back room.

"What happened?" he blurted, alarmed and out of breath. "Are you all right?"

"You won't believe what I just did," I confessed, wincing. "They're going to laugh me to scorn. I can't face anyone."

"They said you ran from a grasshopper?"

Even he could not believe that report.

"No, not a grasshopper. It was a big, hairy spider. That little kid was holding it in his hand." I shuddered at the thought. "I was going to put an *ero* into a jar, but it wasn't a grasshopper and it actually jumped at me."

I buried my face in the palms of my hands.

I had asked some children to help me collect *ero* (pronounced "eh-dough"). *Ero* was, I thought, the word for
grasshopper. Since insects, particularly all shapes and
sizes of grasshopper, swarmed everywhere all the time
in great numbers, I figured if you can't lick 'em, then collect 'em. I went ahead giving each child ten *toea* (equivalent to ten cents) for a specimen that was reasonably
intact, in hopes of mounting each on a little straight pin
and building a colorful collection. The endless variety
fascinated our whole family.

The child who brought me the *ero* that morning had
been unaware of the distinction the larger world makes
between six-legged and eight-legged creatures, not to
mention my own personal distinction, which was rather
meaningful to me. I either ruined Baro's day or gave him
a story to tell around the fire pit for many a year to come.

Moments later, as the memory of my screams replayed
in my head, I cringed with embarrassment.

"I'll never live this one down," I said to my family, and
despaired of returning to the front door and the incred-
ulous villagers.

Neil stood in for me.

"In America," he explained from the porch, "there are
spiders that look like this one, and if they bite you, you'll
die." Graciously he did not mention that I react this way
to all spiders.

By the time I had the nerve to go to the door again myself, a sympathetic group remained, saying, "*Koneo*, Heto
Hama" ("Sorry"), and assuring me that this *ero* would
not kill anybody.

"Look," exclaimed Baro's father as he played with the
now half-dead spider. He held it up in front of my face.

Even given its semiconscious state, I was not going
to risk a closer look.

Owarape Ali jumped up to the porch step. Shaking
his fist and threatening the children, he yelled, "Never

scare the red woman again. Don't you know there are *ero* in America that kill people?"

As a result of this incident, I found out that the fuller meaning of *ero* is "edible six- to eight-legged animal." In the Folopa scheme of things, the number of legs was not as significant as whether or not it could be used for food.

The idea of eating spiders had never really occurred to me before. Perhaps they thought I was collecting them to eat. (Why else would anyone want *ero?*)

What was a person terrified of all insects and spiders trying to prove living in the middle of a tropical rain forest teeming with the biggest, baddest bugs in the whole world? I kept trying to remind myself that I had made this decision.

I hearkened once again to the informal "ceremony" in the director's office where Neil and I had committed to this task, for better or for worse. I remembered his asking if I was aware of the possible difficulties. I hoped, of course, that most of the experiences would be in the *better* category. Alas, the *worse* column was beginning to fill in, with bugs and spiders coming somewhere near the top of the list. Added to all this, the Folopa people knew I was afraid of something as ridiculous as a spider.

My introduction had begun almost immediately with the giant cockroach. But this was not to be my only enemy. In the bug arena were the ones Neil and I called "rain bugs." These little guys waited until it rained (which was often) to come out of somewhere (nobody knew where) and they were attracted to light. As our house at night looked like a veritable lighthouse at the edge of an ocean of dark forest, every rain bug around set a direct course for it.

Resembling small flying ants, they seemed to have no trouble getting into the house. On a particularly bad night, thousands upon thousands of them swarmed around our heads. We had no choice but to turn out the lights and go to bed. The next morning I would sweep the entire house and throw dustpans full of them out the window.

Then there were the nights when moths of every size, shape and color suddenly appeared. Or occasionally it was red stinkbugs. Something about the combination of sun during the day and heavy rain at night brought these to life.

The bug night that crowned them all was *boro ero* night. A *boro ero* is only a brown, grasshopper-like insect with sharp claws on the ends of its legs. It looks innocuous, constantly changing location, flying from the wall, to the floor, to the sink, to my skirt. But unfortunately, for reasons known only to their Creator, they like to crawl inside clothing, and have been known with the proper provocation to bite. And it is hard to imagine not being provoked when a hand on the other side of the garment is tearing at it and screaming, "Get it out, Mommy!" My children began to develop fond childhood memories of chasing down *ero* and passing them out the door or window, where anxious hands waited to cook and eat them for supper.

Fortunately, these nuisance bugs came out in the evening, so I had all day to psyche myself up.

Cockroaches, however, jumped out of cupboards and holes at almost any time. These pests came in two basic sizes: large and extra-large. I did scientific studies on cockroach eggs that bore depressing results. For the large variety, one egg yielded four new roachlettes. The extra-large type produced no fewer than eighteen. For someone of my culture who could not comfortably allow cockroaches to live in her home, this was distressing news.

Another annoying creature was the *nisili sale*. These shiny black millipedes glided slowly up and down the walls from their feeding places in the sago-leaf thatched roof. It was hard to decide which was worse—the noxious odor they emitted or their droppings, which rained down continually and, after accumulation, resembled coffee grounds.

Putting up with insects was exasperating, but nothing made my skin crawl more than a spider. They would leap on me from holes, slide down thread poles in front of my face, scamper like a feather across my bare feet, submit to being delimbed by a child sitting next to me in church, even turn up crumpled in a little heap in my bed. Hiking up a trail once, I came within a handbreadth of walking directly into what, spanning some twelve inches, I was sure was the biggest spider known to man. Later, when I saw the movie *Arachnophobia,* I recognized all the leading spiders.

I tried unsuccessfully to overcome my fear of bugs and spiders. The next-best strategy, I decided, was to look as if I had overcome my fear.

One day I was hoping to demonstrate what an old hand I was getting to be at dealing with the granddaddy bug of them all, called *yǫ uu.* Before that fateful day I had killed and preserved quite a few of these thick-bodied walkingstick bugs. Of all the bugs I had ever seen, this one was the most unique. About six inches in length, it was covered with brown plates, thorns and bumps. It had a head that turned with eyes that followed a moving object.

This particular specimen was brought by a young boy who handed me a branch on which the creature had fastened itself. I could see the insect clearly on the limb, so there would be no surprises. I thought it would be impressive if I managed to get it into a large canning jar by myself, all the while showing no fear.

As I lowered the section of branch gently into the opening of the jar, the creature jumped. It all happened so fast. I saw it coming and thought I would brush it away before it attached itself to me. I dropped the jar, grabbed my skirt and gave it a shake. The timing was perfect. Instead of landing on the outside of my skirt, it hit the underside as the fabric came up. Instantly, as the thought occurred to me that it would find its next perch somewhere on my bare leg, an involuntary and pro-longed wail of anguish came out of my mouth. I began jumping up and down as I yelled and flicked wildly at my skirt, trying to dislodge the bug. The first toss prob-ably sent him across the room, but I kept it up for sev-eral seconds just to make sure.

The escapee was quickly recaptured. I tried to com-pose myself but it was too late. Everyone in the vicinity even vaguely aware of what was happening broke into hysterical laughter.

Was I now to become nothing more than someone to laugh at? Who would take me seriously or think I had anything to offer in this ministry?

It was true that there were places in the world where hairy tarantulas leaped across rooms and cockroaches as big as bedroom slippers glided along floors in the night. Thank the Lord, I had not run into any of those! But I was married to Superman. How could I ever be Superwoman with my phobias? Humble creatures of God's creation were nibbling away at the image I had hoped to portray.

It was impossible to hide my shortcomings, so there was no choice but to appear before everyone as just what I was—weak and fearful.

Darkness and Deep Shadows

Justice is far from us, and righteousness does
not reach us. We look for light, but all is darkness;
for brightness, but we walk in deep shadows.

                                        Isaiah 59:9

The call came down the ridge, passed from man to man—the long, drawn-out *"Whị sukanepooó."*

The village hotline was at work. As the yell was passed along, bone-thin dogs picked up the lament with a high-pitched, sad howl. Soon the small grouping of houses was buzzing with the news: "A man has died at Kẹlamete."

This was a first for Neil and me—the first death since we had come to Fukutao village and the first time we had been this close to real death, the kind with no make-up, satin pillows or flowers.

Wondering about the proper etiquette at such a time, we hoped to take our cues from others who were going to pay their respects. As we would have done in our home culture, Neil and I and our two children ascended the hill somberly and quietly to the hamlet of Kẹlamete.

Some young women walked just ahead of us, giggling and joking as they proceeded up the winding path. How could they be so cheerful when one of their relatives had just died?

The long, narrow "men's house" where the men of Ke̦lamete slept came into view. We stopped to catch our breath and watch the two young women to see what they would do. Instantly they were transformed from chatting friends into loud, wailing mourners. I was shocked. How could they change moods so quickly? They were not faking; these were real tears and genuine sorrow.

We approached slowly. The wailing grew louder.

A great mob of crying men, women and children were bent toward the center of the open area of the men's house. The lifeless form of the deceased lay on the ground; everyone crowded in as close as possible. The next of kin anointed their loved one as they knelt beside him—tears, nasal mucus and saliva dripping freely from their faces.

The contrast between this scene and my own customs of neat-and-clean was so striking that I was at a loss even to categorize the experience. This was grotesque and raw. The horror of death was all too vivid; there could be no denial of reality. The fluids of life and death that we so meticulously wipe away and keep out of sight were here touched and even embraced. How long had my people worked at eliminating all the mess and filth that was now displayed so blatantly before me?

Momako, who was not a close relative, so was not actively mourning, saw Neil's and my looks of puzzlement as we stood there.

"The man's ghost will know how much he was loved," he explained, "and will be happy. He was a very powerful man. We don't want the ghost to be unhappy so that it stays around to make trouble."

So the Folopa wanted the departing spirit to know he was being well-treated. An offended spirit, they believed, could cause sickness and even the death of those who did not mourn sufficiently. As a result of the fear of such consequences, their sorrow was intensely dramatized to have its maximum effect on the ghost.

Out in front of the building, people were clearing away from the area where I was standing. A man with a look of intelligent cunning came forward holding a short section of bamboo. It was the *isi whi̧,* or shaman. With a bold and dramatic gesture he spit into the tube. Other men followed his example. Continuing to watch as I stood close to the entrance to the house, I became aware of someone pulling lightly on my arm and whispering, "Step back, Heto Hama."

The shaman chanted something like a prayer and raised his arms toward the building where the dead man lay. Just as I moved out of the way, the contents of the bamboo were sent showering over the house.

I had read that in the Territory of Papua and New Guinea, before there were Western educators to teach other ideas, the people came up with their own explanations of premature death. When someone died, the cause was seldom thought to be only the result of disease. Beliefs about sorcery were universal on the island, having been passed down generation to generation for thousands of years. Nationwide the practices varied from one group to the next, but all had the same basic themes.

The task of determining the cause of death was given the shaman. In the short period from the time of death until burial, he would perform rituals to pinpoint the culprit and carry out yet another of the never-ending rounds of revenge. In days of old, a full-scale cannibalistic attack might have been ordered, but by the 1970s such attacks were illegal. Modern "payback" was mostly of the supernatural variety.

The saliva shower had been part of the final rituals performed for this powerful man. As a result the ghost of the departed would be "managed" to prevent it from doing harm to others; and someone would pay for the untimely death.

The dead body was wrapped in bark cloth and slung on a pole. Pallbearers lifted the load carefully, making sure all was balanced before departing for the gravesite. Out of the end of the bark shroud, a pair of dusty feet flopped and soon disappeared from view as the carriers did their work quickly.

"This isn't the way we used to do it," said Naniae's grandfather, who lingered behind to reminisce about the old days. "We used to build a high rack and place the body on top. Women sat close by to keep the flies away until the flesh became like liquid. After it was cooked the women ate it. The bones were carefully cleaned and saved so we could use them to contact the spirit of the dead man. With the bones we could find out for sure who it was who killed him."

I could hardly believe what I was hearing. We had spent no more than twelve months in the village so far. This was all so new to us, it was hard to take in. Feeling a little queasy, I suggested we head in the direction of the actual burial site.

We followed the crowd and came to a spot not far from the house. On a steep section of ground where no gardens could be kept, a shallow grave had been dug and lined with sheets of bark.

At the appropriate time, when the body had been positioned properly in the boxlike grave and the bark used for a lid was about to be placed over it, the wife wailed one last time as she threw herself over her dead husband. The helpers pulled her away and the grave was filled in.

A month later Neil went off with the village men on an overnight hunting trip. Heather, Danny and I would be in the house by ourselves. Hariso Hama stood before me with both hands on my arms.

"I will come and stay with you so you won't be lonely," she declared. "When our husbands leave, we cry every night until they return." An unmistakable twinkle of humor shone in her eyes.

The women standing nearby laughed with her. Joining in the fun, they asked me, "Will you cry for your husband tonight?" More giggles.

Not knowing what else to say, I replied, "Yes, I will cry." This was hysterically funny to them.

That evening was a language lesson to remember. Hariso's mother and I sat cross-legged in the living room together over a bowl of popcorn. She was squirming with the excitement of imparting vital information about who was who in Fukutao village. How I wished I could understand everything she wanted me to know! But since the main verbs were the already-familiar *marry, pregnant, born* and *died,* I managed to follow most of it.

There was something about lying over a round log to bring on early labor, and husbands abusing their wives because they refused to become pregnant. Korokoroame had gotten pregnant and was not married so they made her marry Hapale. They were related to each other on the father's side so the marriage was a bad one. They should have been related on the mother's side and then it would have been O.K. Then Kokoame was beaten by her husband for trying to prevent a pregnancy. They say she chewed ginger root and prayed to the spirits. Hariso Hama said this rolling her large, brown eyes back and forth as if someone might be listening to our highly confidential conversation.

"How many children do you have?" I asked, even though I knew the answer. I wanted to hear more about her family.

She stared at me eyeball to eyeball and nose to nose and began her tale. Thanks to her animated style, I was able to understand only too well.

"I married the first time the father of Nare. I didn't choose him. No, but my clan chose him for me. Then I got a baby girl."

At this point she put one fist on top of the other and held them out in front of her. "I did not want that girl so I strangled her and threw her away." A twisting motion of her hands before my eyes illustrated her point graphically.

Looking into her face, I tried not to show my horror. Time seemed to stand still as I glanced down at her hands still held out toward me in a twisted position.

Hariso Hama wrinkled her nose and shook her head, but was otherwise all smiles and enthusiasm as she went on telling me about births and deaths. She accompanied each description with the appropriate dramatics so I would not miss the meaning. She went on to describe her first husband's death and her remarriage, then another list of babies born since then. Most of them still survived. There were girls, Hariso and Meri, and boys, Futo and Filipi.

"Did you—ah, kill any more babies?" I asked as I repeated her twisting gesture, hoping she would not be offended by my question.

"Oh, no," she shot back with a touch of self-righteousness. "We don't do that anymore."

I tried to grasp her reply. Had they really stopped? I had seen no one with birth defects, and it seemed that there should be at least a few in the population. Perhaps the infants they had killed were physically deformed.

"Why did you kill your baby?" I asked timidly.

"I didn't want it," was her lighthearted reply.

I was relieved when my neighbor finally left. My evening had started out like a soap opera on television and had deteriorated to the Halloween horror special. And why did I have such an overdeveloped ability to picture all these things taking place?

The image of Hariso Hama strangling her newborn daughter stayed in my mind. What had this place been

like when they killed not only babies but men, women
and children, and then ate them?

Several days later there was a commotion out in front
of our house. Some villagers had gathered to gossip about
the latest happening. The head man's niece, Somono, was
very ill, perhaps dying. Neil and I could see a small group
of people huddled around the open area in front of a tiny
house a short distance away and wondered if there was
anything we could do to help.

We moved closer and overheard bits of conversation
from the little knots of women who whispered contemp-
tuously. The dialogue was hard to follow but key words
became apparent. *Baby, sharp stick* and *great amounts of
blood* were the ones that struck me as meaningful.

Somono, who appeared to be about fourteen years old,
was not married and most likely had been pregnant. Now
she lay on the ground in the covered open area in front
of her house. Relatives gathered around to determine if
it was serious enough to begin the death wail. Who was
the female culprit who had "helped" this young girl solve
the dilemma with a sharp stick? No one was confessing.

Propped up from behind in her brother's arms, Somono looked unconscious. Her mother sat beside her,
chanting and pulling at the air in front of her face trying to pull away the evil spirits.

The head man approached and begged us to tell him
what was wrong with his niece. Couldn't he hear what
the women were saying? They did not seem to be trying
to hide either their diagnosis or their feelings about their
young neighbor.

"She has been poisoned!" he insisted. "Someone is
trying to kill her. She'll die if we don't kill her pig."

The shedding of the animal's blood was thought to distract the enemy spirit forces. It was hoped that these forces
would take the animal's soul and leave the human alone.

After a small pig had been wrestled into position, the head man grabbed a wooden club and struck the animal on its forehead, killing it instantly. I wondered if this was the same pig whose eyes had been gouged out the month before in front of our house. That, I had learned, was a common practice to prevent pigs from running away. I was glad pigs were not particularly cute and that this one's end was fairly quick and painless.

With typical Folopa dexterity, the head man produced a sharp knife and cut the animal open. Hacking off a piece of the liver, he roasted it quickly over a fire. When it had cooked sufficiently, Somono's mother tweaked off tiny pieces to insert into her mouth.

The *isi whį* arrived and made his way through the small crowd of people. As he smoked his long bamboo pipe and crouched before the sacrificial pig, he closed his eyes and looked as if he was in a trance. Before long the shaman's verdict was in: Someone in a neighboring village was working sorcery on the girl. The rituals of counter-sorcery would be performed as soon as there were no distractions.

Neil and I took the hint and left.

As we walked home, my head reeled with images of death and dying, blood and gore. There was no retreat, except in our house (where I faced only spiders, dirty diapers and occasionally burned bread), from the realities of a life filled, as Isaiah wrote millennia ago, with darkness and deep shadows.

The more we learned of the culture and people, the more the facts overwhelmed me. How harsh their world was for them! My natural instinct was to change something. I wanted to bring some kind of relief for the suffering and hope to the hearts that seemed to carry only fear. But at this early stage Neil and I were the learners. We had to understand what was going on and to speak the language adequately, so the truths of the Bible would make sense to them and be accurate.

How frustrated I felt to see so much need and be able to do so little! But I knew provision of material comforts would be only a temporary solution, not to mention how impossible it would be to try to meet the needs of the thousands of others who lived in this rain forest. What they needed most was not material; it was spiritual—the truth that was found in the Bible, written in their language.

It would be another year or two before we knew enough to begin the actual work of Bible translation. Would we have to just plod on with our learning, waiting to tell them the good news of Jesus Christ?

For me there was always a tension in my relationship to the Folopa people. I imagined that they looked at me and saw a privileged foreigner who had unlimited resources and few worries. I wanted to gather them all in front of me and explain in fluent Folopa that I was sorry for the apparent inequities.

I was not able to do that. In the meantime, I had to face them every day, keenly feeling the extreme differences in our lives.

A Very Great Punishment

"Is it nothing to you, all you who pass by? Look around and see. Is any suffering like my suffering that was inflicted on me. . . . ?"

Lamentations 1:12

I heard a rustling sound, then an unmistakable clearing of the throat. Someone was standing outside the front door trying to get my attention with the Folopa custom equivalent to our knocking. "Heto Hama, you must come quickly."

Opening the door, I saw Akaya, a quiet young man, a serious and devout member of the local church. Now he looked anxious and fearful.

"You must come now. My wife is dying."

As Akaya reported this, I knew he was wrong. The man's wife was only in labor, and the time had come for the birth of the baby.

"I'm coming," I replied as I rubbed on some insect repellent and grabbed my flashlight.

Fopeame was a shy young woman. She had stood on the porch with some other young people watching me work in my kitchen. I had noticed that she was close to giving birth, and had asked if I could be there when the

baby was born so I could learn about the ways of Folopa
childbirth. A look of amused embarrassment had passed
over Fopeame's face but she had said yes. First babies
often died, along with their mothers, and no doubt it
was good insurance to have someone with the knowledge of the red man's medicine present.

Ducking inside the low opening of the improvised
shelter, I seated myself on the dirt with the other women
and the midwife. The pole-and-bark building, offering
nothing more than privacy and retreat from the rain,
had been constructed for this occasion. It would be torn
down in a day or two, making sure every trace of the
event had been removed.

A small fire gave just enough light to see Fopeame
kneeling to face the corner post, exhausted and sweat-
ing profusely. Her hands gripped the post in front of her.
If I had not been there, most likely she would have been
naked, but now a bark cape was draped from the top of
her head. Several banana leaves waited to catch the
falling newborn.

"Sukuyaalopó—sae! Sae!" the midwife, an older woman, pleaded from where we all huddled. ("You will
die—push! Push!")

Then the midwife began to tell me the ways of Folopa
women.

"We women have to sit here and tell her to push hard.
If she doesn't push during the whole time of labor, the
baby will not find the path. See that hard place?" she
asked, pointing to the girl's upper abdomen. "That is the
head of the baby. She has to push so it will turn over and
come out head first. If it comes feet first, she will die.
We can't let her forget. We must instruct her during the
whole time of pain."

Quietly gripping the post with renewed determination, Fopeame bore down again as the next contraction
contorted her body. After a couple more of the same, I
noticed a small pile of feces right where the baby was

due to land. Just as I pointed this out to the midwife, a baby boy dropped unceremoniously head-first right into the filth.

My first thought was to lunge for him and clean him off. Instead everyone sat silent and still, waiting.

"Are you going to pick him up?" I whispered.

"Oh, no. We can't do that. We have to wait to see if he is alive."

"He *is* alive. He's moving his arms and legs. Pick him up," I pleaded.

"When he breathes, then we know he is alive," she replied calmly.

I could hear the struggle for breath, a gurgling and rasping in the little throat.

Are we going to sit here and watch this baby die? I screamed in my mind. Sitting helplessly beside the women, I willed the child to cough, and held my own breath until the tiny infant fought clear of the phlegm and let his outrage be known. No one else seemed very concerned.

"He is alive. We are happy."

Everyone was smiling, and I was drained and weak with relief.

While the baby lay still untouched, they continued to chat and tell me about their most tragic childbirth horror stories. What effect this had on the new mother, I could only guess. Then I remembered it was not much different where I came from.

After the placenta was lying safely in a mass beside the boy, he was picked up and dissevered from it. A tiny bowl of water and small sponge were used to dab away the obvious blood and other contaminants.

As the midwife finished cleaning up, she proudly explained even more. "Now we know how to deliver babies the right way. Before we didn't do it this way. When the pains began, we were made to go out of the village. In the dark, in the rain, with no shelter, we went out behind our houses in the weeds to have the babies. We were alone with no one to help."

They shook their heads, looking at the ground, as if to say, "How could we ever have done that?"

Having had two children in a nice, safe hospital delivery room, I could not imagine such an experience.

Fopeame was now lying on her side beside the fire, while her mother held the baby admiringly. Looking into her face, I could tell she was in pain, but she did not complain. In fact, she had never made a sound during the whole ordeal.

I returned to my house after promising Fopeame's husband some pain tablets to take back to the new mother. I thought over all that I had heard about the past and had observed in the present. Childbirth was not the nightmare it had been before the Folopa had learned to do it the "right" way, but it was still filled with trauma and risk. The mortality rate for both mothers and children was high.

☙   ☙

"Heto Hama." Akaya sidled up to me the next day and spoke bashfully. "What shall I name the child? Is there a Bible name for him?"

I was surprised that the new father was asking me to choose a name. Normally babies were not named so soon, and they were not really considered to be human beings until at least a month old. Although the villagers knew little at this time of the actual content of the Bible, they knew it was supposed to be God's Book. Did they think Bible names were good omens for survival, perhaps having some magical power to protect? I did not know. But I considered quickly which Bible names were already being used in the village and came up with one.

"Joshua," I said, not even remembering that the Folopa do not have a *j* sound in their language.

Akaya smiled humbly, repeated the name as best he could, then turned and headed back to his wife and child.

❧ ❧

Backbreaking garden work, pregnancies and births, nursing one baby after another, cuts and sores, blood and pus and mud, pain and sorrow. Life for women in the rain forest was not fun. Being there watching them suffer was not fun either.

My life was so different from theirs. My activities were performed almost entirely in the house. Theirs were all physical labors done outside the house. When I did my work, aside from household chores, it was mostly sitting down at a desk.

"Your wife is like a man," Hariso's uncles told Neil once.

"Why is that?" he replied curiously.

"For one, she doesn't smell. All our women smell bad. Also, you talk to her. When we are trying to make an important decision, we ask our brothers. You ask your wife. Next, she knows how to do things. Our women know only how to weed the garden and plant sweet potato."

They had also noted from our home tours that Neil and I not only lived in the same house but slept in the same bed, yet Neil's strength was not sapped by the constant female presence. In their thinking, men and women must live separately in order for men to maintain their maleness. Any contact with one's wife must take place away from the village, where contamination from her could be left behind. Women could be very dangerous, but apparently I was not having too bad an effect on Neil. This was a source of wonder.

When Neil passed on these observations to me, at first I laughed. The more I thought about it, however, the more I could see I really was different.

We had been sitting on the bench back in Port Moresby when Neil had asked Mosa about the possibility of hiking from Erave, the airstrip closest at the time to the Folopa-speaking people, to Fukutao village.

"How many days does it take to walk there?" he asked.

Mosa gave it careful thought. "For a Folopa, I think two days," he said in Pidgin. "For a white man, I think three days."

"How many days for my wife?"

Mosa looked at me, no doubt considering the severe illness I had just come through. "I think fourteen days," he replied.

The message was clear to me: White women are marshmallows. Mosa's expectations of my performance in the bush were lower than low. On a scale of one to ten, I registered about minus three.

I kept trying, though. I knew I had to keep working on relating to the Folopa people, differences or no. So one day I told Baro's father that I wanted to go work in the garden. Since I had never been there, I could only imagine what it was like getting there, somewhere at the end of a pointed finger where all I could see was mountains and dense vegetation. "*Upaae*," they said, which meant, "Way over there."

Baro Ali was sure he had heard me wrong. The very idea that I could even get to his garden, let alone be of any help, brought a look of horror to his face. But I detected a glint of laughter as well. What was he thinking? I imagined he was picturing me slipping and sliding up and down muddy slopes, fainting dead away at the sight of blood running down my leg from leech bites, and lying in an exhausted heap at the bottom of the valley at the end of the day, too tired to climb back up to the village.

I wanted to prove him wrong but the odds were not in my favor. I did know one thing—that I had to descend into the valley off the north side of Fukutao's ridge location. The trouble was, I had no idea how far it was to the bottom of the valley, let alone back up the other side.

I spent much of the journey to the garden trying to skirt mud puddles. I was bitten by insects, stuck with thorns and scraped on rocks, all in an attempt to avoid stepping in mud. From this I eventually concluded that the best way to cope with mud is to lie down in the first mud hole you come to. Then it is best to turn over three or four times to be sure all surfaces are covered. Get up, pluck off any odd leeches that think they are in for a free meal, and proceed down the trail. At this point you will have nothing else to worry about.

Once we arrived at the steep mountainside garden, I was not much use for work, and my family-for-a-day knew it. I looked every bit of the "red" woman that I was, thoroughly flushed from the exertion. I offered to help but they merely laughed and went about their business of weeding and digging up sweet potato.

I marveled that such terrain could actually produce food crops. It certainly did not look like a garden in the sense of any I had ever seen. There were no neat rows of plants, but a random mix of tuberous plants, sugar cane, squash and other vegetables I did not recognize. Huge trees had been felled perhaps years before and, too large to cut up and move, were left lying. Stacks of pulled-up and dried undergrowth were piled next to the trees to make room for plants.

Each member of the family knew just what to do. The children pulled weeds while the mother bent over from the hips and thrust her sharp digging stick into the ground to locate the tubers. After she was sure of a find, she scraped away the soil with her fingers and pulled it from the ground. Hands would be washed off later (there was no running water up on the ridge) when my companions reached the stream at the bottom of the valley at the end of the day.

Again I marveled that they worked in the garden several times a week without fail. The only other option was hunger.

Baro's mother teased me unmercifully as we contemplated our return trip to the village. "Husband, we will have to make a shelter for Heto Hama to spend the night. Remember the time she fell off the trail and landed upside down?"

She laughed out loud. Her husband merely looked at me with pretended sympathy.

I was not sure if this was in the same vein as the teasing Neil took the first time he was invited on a hunting trip. They had taunted him, "We are going a long way into the bush, but you probably couldn't make it"—a remark they knew would provoke him into action. Now it was my turn.

Later that afternoon, as they sat down to rest before heading back to the village, Baro's cousin Kepawhiso offered me some steamed caterpillars from a bamboo she pulled out of her string bag. I decided to be brave and eat one. As that rubbery little smoked snack slid down my throat, I figured it would be worth it for all the affirmation I would now receive. Surely the women would take this as a sign that I was trying to relate to their ways.

Kepawhiso was not impressed.

I ate a second one.

"Do you want another one?" she asked hesitantly, probably noticing the lack of pure pleasure on my face.

I tried to act as if I really had to stop and think about the decision. "No."

"That's right. You'd better not eat any more or you might throw up. Red people like you should not eat strange food they're not used to."

I thought grumpily about the hero's welcome Neil had received on returning from that hunting trip, having eaten all kinds of Folopa *hors d'oeuvres*. For that reason I had now half-expected tickertape to shower down on me from overhead. All I got was "You might throw up."

Barely had I recovered from my disappointment when Kepawhiso stroked my blouse and said, "Look at your clothes. There are no holes, no stains."

I forced a smile and agreed with her.

"Look at our clothes—old, worn. We can't even mend our dresses because we have no *kepi*."

Kepi or vine was their word for our thread. It was an obvious hint that it would be good if I donated some of my thread to the cause, since they had been so nice to take me along that day. Their dresses were badly worn since most had begun as used clothing in the first place, purchased from distant trade stores.

They were right, of course. I *was* better off than they were—by a long shot. But it made me feel uncomfortable to be reminded. Then, instead of merely making a mental note to give them some thread when we returned, I went off on a mental guilt trip. Again my thoughts hammered away at my estimation of my performance as a missionary. I had so much more. I was a privileged character. How could I relate to these people when we were so different? I was failing in my efforts to bridge the gap between us, even with this trip to their gardens. Suddenly I wished I were somewhere else, just to get away from the awful reality. Could I ever do a good job of being a missionary?

Baro's mother grabbed my hand and held it up to her face. (Because she was a tiny woman, that was not very high.)

"Look at your hands," she said. "No calluses, no scars and so clean. Look at our hands—covered with cuts, dirt that won't wash off, callused from digging in our gardens. We have a big punishment to endure."

I had heard this statement often. What did it mean? Did they think God had forgotten them? That He was punishing them for not being good enough by making their lives so unspeakably hard? Could I tell them this was not true? What *was* the truth?

Sometimes I asked myself the same question. Were these people punishing me with all their comments about what I had that they did not have? Or was it God punishing me because I was not the person I should be, or because I had the wrong values? It was like a punishment every day to be reminded of all my terrible shortcomings—before the people and, worst of all, before God Himself.

"You are right," I said to Baro's mother.

I did not know what else to say.

With the work finished for the day, we trudged back down the mountain across the valley and up the long, steep trail to the top of the ridge. I carried a walking stick and hoped I would make it before I died. Baro's mother carried a string bag full of sweet potatoes that weighed more than she did, arriving home slowly and painstakingly from just another day at the garden.

I waited for some congratulations, but of course going to the garden was no big deal to anyone but me.

Meanwhile, at my house, it was time to get back to work in the kitchen. Spectators had gathered to discuss what that big lump of white stuff was that I was pushing and pounding on. There was constant speculation about how many spoons I owned, and were we really going to eat that brown, yucky-looking stuff, and why did the meat not rot inside that tin?

I wanted to answer their questions but, in addition to not knowing the language very well, I just did not know what to say.

"Yes, I know I have a lot of spoons, but I need them, really." *Or do I?*

"No, this brown stuff is not what you think it is. It's chocolate pudding and it tastes quite good."

"The meat doesn't rot because the bacteria in the tin has been killed by heat." *How do I explain bacteria?*

As I prepared dinner that evening, dark clouds poured in over the ridge to the south. There was always a warning before the rain began. I could see the heavy clouds approach through my window high on the ridge. Soon a wall of water was roaring up the valley toward the village. I was filled with sympathy for the women who had stayed late to get the most of the daylight hours to weed and dig up yams and taro.

At dusk they began to return, loaded down with garden produce. They were tired, muddy, leech-bitten, hungry, bent from aching backs. They were coming home to hungry, cranky children and cold, dark huts. By the time they passed by my window, they were soaked to the skin, despite the three-foot-wide taro leaves to cover their heads and the loads they bore from the downpour.

I stood comfortably at my sink and called out the window, "*Hamao, Koneo.* [Sister, greetings.] Where have you come from?"

I now knew that this, and not *Good morning* or *Good afternoon*, was the proper thing to say to a passerby. In fact, *koneo* was the word for both *Greetings* and *I'm sorry*, and came from the root word for *compassion*. So when the Folopa said, "Greetings," they were saying, "Compassion to you."

"*Koneo*, Heto Hama. I've come from the garden with this heavy load."

"I'm sorry. It's dark and cold," I said, feeling sorry for both of us—for her because of the hardship, and for me because of the discomfort of facing her when I was warm and fed.

"That's right. You stay in your warm house and sleep while I go, cold and wet, to my house to feed my hungry children. I have a great punishment to endure," she added.

I bit my lip and, once again, did not know how to respond.

A Matter of Life and Death

"Have I not wept for those in trouble? Has not my soul grieved for the poor?"

Job 30:25

A high, thin wail from the other side of the wall pierced the midnight darkness and woke me from a sound sleep. Waking Neil up, I said, "Kepa Ali must have died. His father is mourning."

Neil and I jumped out of bed, dressed hastily and rushed out into our living room to see our overnight guests gathered around what was now a corpse. Neil knelt down and listened to the dead man's chest. Silence. We looked at each other in disbelief.

"You'd better go tell everyone," I said.

Neil opened the window and yelled, "Hariso Ali. Kepa Ali has died."

"Eh, what?" came the stammering reply from inside our near neighbor's house, as Erima apparently struggled to wake himself.

"Kepa Ali is dead. You'd better tell the others."

There was a mumble of voices as the family was roused and told of the death. Then the old man pulled away the bark door and stumbled out into the wet night air. Standing in the middle of the path facing Kęlamete hamlet, he cupped his hands to his mouth and yelled, *"Whį sukanepooó."* Turning to the opposite direction, he hollered out to the nearer houses.

Within minutes, mourning men and women streamed into our house, filling every inch of space. Pandemonium reigned.

Fighting my way to the children's bedroom through the tangle of bodies, I tried to make myself heard over the uproar to explain the disturbance to Heather and Danny. They had been asleep in their bedroom just a few feet away and were now wide awake. It was impossible to be heard, so I pushed back through the crowd once again and shouted to Neil, "Have them take the body to his house."

Neil stood on a chair and yelled out the request. Quick compliance, and the group shifted and flowed out the door like a giant amoebae. Slowly the noise died away. The children were tucked into bed once again, and we sat in the silence staring into the embers of the fire, trying to make some sense out of this turn of events.

It had been only two days before that Kepa Ali had come to our door holding up his swollen hand. He was a quiet man with kind eyes. Gently he informed me that as he was reaching into a ground hole to retrieve an escaping rodent, a snake had bitten him. "If you don't give me medicine, I'll die."

Since he had been bitten the day before and was still able to stand and explain things, I felt perhaps he was wrong. We had been told that there were no poisonous snakes in the area—a story that was soon changed.

"We have no medicine for snakebite," I told him.

The words seemed like a death sentence, but Neil and I prayed that Kepa Ali was wrong about what had bitten him.

On the radio transceiver, the doctor said that if Kepa Ali survived for three days, he would probably not die.

It had already been two days since he was bitten. A helicopter was scheduled to come in just two more days, transporting some visitors. It could bring anti-venom medication as well if the patient could just hold onto life that long. We knew this was his only chance, as no other helicopter was available in the whole province.

"My hands and feet are getting cold. I'm going to die," Kepa Ali reported an hour later with a pleading note in his voice. I noticed a slight slur in his speech.

Surely if he lasted this long, I thought, *he can hold on longer.*

Everyone else seemed to believe he would die. We wanted to prove them wrong. We decided to have him sleep in our living room that night to make sure he got food and water.

"Why feed a dead man, Heto Hama?" his relatives asked.

No one believed he would survive.

"He won't die. He's lived almost three days. He can make it one more." I tried to sound confident.

That night Kepa Ali's old father sat at his head and kept watch. A son and other clan members rested close by and tried to believe there was hope, but they, too, were waiting for the inevitable.

When the end came, it was a blow to us.

After he had been carried away, I could picture what must be taking place at Kepa Ali's home, like the harsh scene at the men's house shortly after we came to Fuku-tao village.

Why did it seem as though we worked so hard and prayed so much, yet death still came to those we had tried to help? Was God not listening? Had we done something wrong?

The next day we received some consolation. Kepa Ali's family insisted that no sorcery be done in conjunction with his death. They took a stand to those in the village who did not claim to be Christians, saying that they would ask God to show them the purpose for his death.

It was encouraging to see the message of the Bible, with few portions having actually been translated and taught so far, affecting lives in such a positive way.

Still, the death seemed like a defeat. I had been sure that if we demonstrated enough faith, a miracle would happen. My faith and my efforts seemed to count for nothing.

🐾   🐾

Medicine was a field that had never attracted me. It was like torture for me to see people suffer and, most of all, die. I had taken the medical training in Mexico but given little thought to what it would be like living in a place where I would be called on to render such service, and see such dismal results.

In the territory of Papua and New Guinea (which had become the independent nation of Papua New Guinea by the end of our first four-year term of service), many village locations had access to some kind of medical care. Folopa land was not one of them. No one ever said we had to help the village in this way. Rather, we had seen the suffering and decided there was no choice.

After seeing abscessed teeth, bush knife cuts, malaria and a couple of deaths, we left the village for our time at Ukarumpa and went shopping at the center clinic for a good supply of medicines and bandaging material. On our next three-month stay, we would make sure to have the basic treatments for all the common ailments and some good medical books to refer to.

My first patient had been Deke, Yoso's eight-month-old son. My knees were knocking as I poised the syringe of penicillin inches from his tiny buttocks. I was afraid Yoso would see how nervous I was. What if the child had a reaction? What if he grew up with a fear of white people because of the pain I was about to inflict? What if I missed the right place on his little behind and crippled him for life?

I aimed and jabbed. His mother smiled confidently at me as her child screamed in pain. *If only she knew.*

The children were the hardest to treat. It took four adults to hold down an active three-year-old when it was time to put any liquid medicine down his or her throat. Only moments before we would think a child was at death's door—but just come at him with a spoon and it was like pouring water on a cat. Before I learned the technique of depressing the tongue to allow gravity a chance to work, I took many a dose in the face. Peanut butter, I discovered, disguises nasty-tasting malaria pills that would never otherwise have a hope of reaching their intended destination.

Parents sat on the front porch awaiting their child's turn. "The *sapata so* [white woman] will put you in jail if you don't stop crying." This threat was supposed to subdue children. All it produced was hysteria.

Adults, on the other hand, endured painful treatments like stoics. They chewed and swallowed bitter malaria pills without even a grimace. The nastier the medicine or the more painful its application, the more beneficial it had to be. If it came from us, they believed it would help—even when the problem was beyond our expertise.

One day as I was up to my elbows in bread dough, I looked out my kitchen window and saw a woman crawling down the path toward our house. Slowly and painstakingly she worked her way along the ground.

Seeing Hariso Hama sitting on the ground in front of her house, I called out, "What is wrong with that woman? Is there no one to carry her?"

My neighbor looked up and said in a disinterested manner, "That's a Kęlamete woman."

"Is she sick?"

Hariso Hama glanced up at me with a grin and a mischievous twinkle. "Oh, yes. She's very sick."

This was strange. I thought everyone knew we made house calls anytime, night or day. Why hadn't she sent a message to us? There were people everywhere, yet no one was helping this woman get down the hill. In fact, they were laughing at her.

Not sure of what to do, I walked out and around the side of the house as she approached. Not slowing her pace or acknowledging my presence, she continued until she reached the porch, crawled up the step and collapsed dramatically.

"Sister, what sickness do you have?" I asked.

She motioned to her neck as she mumbled the symptoms. From there her hand moved across to her shoulder, back to her chest, around her abdomen, down to her hips and finally to her knees.

"Bamboo, give me the bamboo," she whispered hoarsely as if about to draw her last breath.

Everyone knew that "bamboo" medicine was very effective. Just about every time someone got penicillin in a glass "bamboo" with the needle attached to the end, they recovered.

I did not know what to make of her symptoms, except that lots of older women complained of the same things. All these women, however, came to me upright. I was fairly sure that penicillin was not needed for this complaint, but what could I say in the face of such apparent severe need?

She seemed to faint with pain when I inserted the needle, then roused some, only to groan and cry.

Once the medicine was administered, there was nothing more I could do for her. As she continued to lie on the porch, I went back to my bread-baking duties. My patient began chatting with another woman who had already returned from her garden for the day and was sitting in the shade of the porch. After about fifteen minutes she jumped to her feet and exclaimed, "Bamboo medicine is very delicious," and took off toward home at a dogtrot.

Seeing this, of course, made me wonder what I had really accomplished with my medical help. Did the woman have a real condition that warranted treatment, or had she been faking sickness in hopes of getting relief for the aches and pains of hard work and age? And why had I given in to her wishes when I knew better than to give an injection that would do her no good, maybe even be harmful in the long run? I knew it was guilt that always reared its head when I was confronted with needs that were impossible for me to meet. I did anything that would make people happy and meet their expectations.

Sometimes it was the patient who knew more than I did. An old man from another village came to my door one day and asked for medicine.

"What is the sickness?" I asked him.

"It is 'body-weak sickness,'" he replied, as if this would be perfectly clear.

It seemed to me that I remembered someone coming just a few weeks before who had complained of a weak body. I thought the complaint had been of the "blood-finished sickness." Could this be anemia, as in Mexico, where *blood finish* means anemia? Why not ask this man about that sickness?

"Is your blood finished?" I asked.

The old man gave me a very strange look and backed away, mumbling something about its not being that sickness. He never came for medicine again.

Later I saw the patient whose blood had been finished. It was a very obviously pregnant woman. Suddenly I realized why the old man had looked at me as if I were crazy. I had probably asked him if he was pregnant.

I had just sat down to lunch with Neil, Heather and Danny after a busy morning running between the schoolroom and the front door. We had seen an unusual number of sick children.

"Whew, what a morning!" I remarked as we sipped our soup *du jour*. "Those people still waiting outside have been there for hours. I even had Joshua's mother come this morning asking for medicine. It didn't seem like anything very critical, though."

A serious cough was going around, however, and half the children in the village had it. At least six-month-old Joshua was healthy and happy, I was glad to see. I still wondered if he would be normal after that traumatic birth.

Suddenly from somewhere out in front of our house came a muffled cry, then a scream of anguish. We all jumped up and piled out the door to see what the problem was. A woman on her hands and knees was pounding the ground and screaming, "My son, my son!" The father was sitting on the ground holding his six-year-old child, who appeared to be sleeping on his lap. As they had sat waiting to be seen by one of us, the boy had died.

We had no idea anyone was waiting who was seriously ill, or we would have checked him earlier. Nor had the parents realized, as all had been quiet in front of our house before that moment.

We tried to console them, but they were in deep grief and shock. I examined the child briefly and asked some questions about his illness. He had had a very bad cough.

We, too, were in shock. This had never happened before. Folopa people are experts on death, knowing very well all the signs as it approached.

Our family gathered at the table again long after our soup had turned cold. It was hard to finish the meal after such a trauma. Were there other children out there just as close to death? Would they die, or would we be able to save them? We did not even know why this child had died so unexpectedly. The same feeling of impotence overcame me.

When I thought things could not get worse, they did. The next day the younger brother of the child who had died met the same fate. Neil had visited them at their house and diagnosed pneumonia only hours before, but it was too late.

It was almost too much to bear.

In all, five children died that week. We called the Papua New Guinea provincial health officer via radio, who dispatched a government doctor on a chartered helicopter. We knew the problem was being taken seriously, as this charter cost the government thousands of kinas (a kina is roughly equivalent to a dollar).

As soon as the doctor arrived, he went straight to work.

"Show me one of the sick children," he said in English, the official language of the country.

"Right over here in the house next to ours," I said, leading him to the open area in front of the house, where two of Hariso Hama's younger children lay on the ground, weak and ill.

The younger boy timed his next coughing spasm perfectly, just as the doctor attended to him.

"Why, these children have whooping cough," he informed us with shock and alarm in his voice. "How can this happen when we sent a patrol around the entire area to vaccinate children against such diseases?"

There were many ways this could have happened, we knew only too well. If families were away from Fukutao village gardening in a remote place, they would not come all the way back simply to receive a kind of medicine for children who did not look sick. In fact, only the extremely sick came to ask for medicine, many waiting until it was too late for any medication to help. Also, it was difficult for the patrols to keep the vaccine cool enough to survive the jungle heat. Warm vaccine was useless.

Having a real doctor in the village felt good. For once the responsibility was shifted from Neil and me. He was an expert and would now diagnose and recommend treatment.

"Are you people registered medical workers?" the doctor asked.

"No, sir, but there is no one else here to help these people, so we do what we can."

"Well, here's what you must do, then," he said with all his doctorly authority. "Each of these sick children must have crystalline penicillin four times a day for the next two weeks. I've brought some along and will leave it with you. It should be enough for the whole village."

I knew it was my missionary duty to serve willingly no matter what the personal cost, but as I calculated what it would take to treat all the sick children, I grew tired thinking about it. The parents would probably not see the importance of getting the medicine at regular intervals. But it had to be done to make sure no one else died.

If I were a good missionary, I pondered to myself, *I would not give any thought to my own needs. Lord, I'm sorry for being so selfish.*

We did the best we could, and no more children died. Two weeks later when the crisis had passed, we were exhausted.

The village was still reeling from the sudden deaths of two children in one family when the next bad news came.

"Heto Hama, my wife is dead," Akaya said, quiet but obviously very distressed.

It had been only six months since I had sat in the birth hut and observed little Joshua's entrance into the world. Fopeame was so young and healthy-looking. How could she be dead?

I thought about how she had come asking for medicine almost in a whisper. Perhaps she had picked up an infection from the birth and was embarrassed to tell me the details. It was too late now to wonder. Now both Akaya and his little son were on their own to survive, as there were no close female relatives to feed the baby.

I asked villagers what I could do to help.

"There's nothing you can do to help," they said. "This happens all the time. Lots of children lose their mothers. It's just the way things are."

My heart ached for a suffering people who did not know that in some parts of the world, it does not happen that way. And in all my missionary fantasies, it did not happen that way even here. The sick person always got well. But the reality for us had been that most of the villagers died.

Was I expecting God to write a script so that we would all live like Cinderella, happily ever after? He could, of course. Why didn't He?

More Bugs

It is not good to have zeal without knowledge,
nor to be hasty and miss the way.

Proverbs 19:2

What I lacked in the way of Folopa bush skills, I had hoped to make up for on the other side of my job description. Surely I had not anguished my way through all those linguistics courses for nothing! Perhaps analyzing the Folopa language would be less humiliating than trying to speak it.

The first task Neil and I had faced after beginning our work with the Folopa language had been to look at all the words we had written down and figure out the letters of the alphabet. We had fourteen vowels and fourteen consonants, with only a few that were difficult to say. Together we wrote a paper describing all the sounds.

Some time after that, during one of our breaks at Ukarumpa, we attended a literacy workshop. There we were taught a step-by-step procedure for producing primers and short story books for teaching the Folopa people how to read their own language.

One week into the four-week course, our third child, Bruce, was born. I missed one week of classes but was there again for the third and fourth weeks. Maternity leave would have to wait.

For those periods when we were in the village, language study and Bible translation were Neil's primary occupation. But as for me, my major task each day was one that my pre-field training had not addressed. From eight in the morning until noon each day, I home-schooled my children.

My short history in this kind of teaching had not been stunning. After one particularly long village stay of five months, in which I taught Heather most of first grade, we returned to Ukarumpa so the teacher could evaluate her progress.

"What has she been doing all this time?" the teacher asked, alarmed at her lack of skill in reading.

"You know," I said apologetically, "Heather just doesn't seem to respond to phonics lessons."

It was true. The activity that occupied most of Heather's time was teaching a group of older girls and women to read in Folopa. The skill she was as yet unable to do herself, she was trying to teach to all she could gather to learn.

But both principal and teacher were positive that dark clouds loomed over my daughter's academic future. Grave warnings were issued and I was sent back to the village next time with piles of remedial reading materials.

Two years later the situation improved only slightly when Danny started school. His problem was boredom. Mine, too. Dan had listened as Heather had read those same books aloud, and now there was little to interest him. We were both yawning long before the morning work was finished.

Spelling lessons did hold a few perks for me. I learned to spell a couple of words I had been misspelling my whole literate life. But both of us sat with glazed eyes as we wearily plugged along.

Later, when Danny was in the third grade, the low point of the week was talking to the classroom teacher on the two-way radio.

"Hello, students. This is Miss Smith with the grade three school broadcast. I'll tell you where we are in each subject and then we'll have the roll call."

I looked around to find my student.

"Forty-two delta papa," she said, reading off the radio call sign. "Are you there, Rebecca? Over."

"Hi, Miss Smith. I've finished all the work this week. Well, actually, I'm two chapters ahead. I've learned all the times tables. Can you please send me 25 more library books on the next flight? I finished the ones you sent last time. Over."

"That's wonderful, Rebecca."

I grimaced.

Miss Smith moved on to the next three students, who reported much the same progress. That was except for Peter, who recited a poem he had written extolling the virtues of his teacher.

"Sixty-eight alpha alpha. Danny, how are you doing? Over."

There was such expectancy in the voice, I hated to disappoint her.

"Hello, Miss Smith. This is Danny's mother. I told him to come in for the radio at four o'clock, but he must have forgotten. Over."

I knew he was probably hiding so he would not have to talk to his teacher. He was painfully shy.

"Do you have any questions about the schoolwork? Over."

"No, we're just fine—not quite up to the others, but no problem. Over."

This was not completely true, but could I say right on the radio where everyone could hear, "No actually, my son hates reading. Right now I'm bribing him just to get through last week's lesson. Please don't send any more library books because the baby ate one yesterday. They're being used mostly as a raceway for Matchbox cars. Over and out!"

Someone, please give me a linguistic project. Teaching is not my forte.

At the beginning, after many months of Folopa language study, Neil began his first attempts at Bible translation. He decided to start with Genesis because, after all, that was the beginning of everything. My part of the task was typing. I spent many long afternoon hours hunched over a manual typewriter named Hermes Ambassador deciphering handwritten hieroglyphics produced in the Bible house and turning out pages of neatly typed text.

When the book of Genesis was finally completed near the end of our first four-year term, I got my biggest assignment yet. I would type the camera-ready copy, which would then go to the printshop at Ukarumpa and be made into a real book.

Rumor had reached my ears that there was a new development at the center: The computer was about to arrive. But the promise of my work becoming easier sounded, in fact, just the opposite. Computers must be very hard to use, I decided. I had heard that people had to go in and take a course just to learn how to operate them.

So I took the risk and continued with my project. I would be finished long before those newfangled boxes took over. In the time it would take to learn how to use the new computer, I would be done typing. For weeks I pressed on, painstakingly producing letter-perfect pages. The stack grew higher and higher, and my self-esteem along with it.

Then the fateful day arrived. Neil came in to announce, "Great news! I gave the copy of Genesis to the computer department, and they've finished typing it already. It's all ready to print! You'll never have to type on that old Hermes again."

The energy started to drain out of my body. I felt my brain turning to jello.

"I don't think I knew this," I said, slumping in the chair. "Did you tell me?"

"No, I thought I'd surprise you."

It was a surprise, all right. All my beautiful pages, now moving sideways, now slipping, now falling into the trash basket, now going up in smoke. Instead of the handwriting being on the wall, it was on the computer screen. Manual typewriters were officially obsolete.

I vowed to learn a lesson from this: When technology moves on, I had better follow.

Not to be undone, I decided to move ahead with determination. This time the challenge was the computer itself.

The method of operation in the new computer department was to give beginners like myself only as much information as was necessary for the task being completed. Any more than this was overwhelming and confusing, as computers at first were not very user-friendly. The large room was arranged so that the beginners were clustered together in one section.

It had not taken long for the computer to catch on. Not only did typists work at every available machine, but there was a waiting list on which time slots were booked to accommodate the many who wanted their translation to be computerized.

The brains of the outfit was a very nice man who went around quietly troubleshooting for all of us computer novices. Poor Alger, who worked at the main desk off to one side, was kept busy from dawn to dusk trying to help everyone on the network.

So when my computer started giving me problems, I hated to bother him. "Alger, I'm sorry. The screen went blank when I turned it on."

He smiled, though a tiny hint of alarm showed in his eyes.

"I don't have any more machines available. Why don't you sit down at the mother computer and work, just until I can see what's wrong with this one?"

Printers were whirring and all noses were to the grind-stone. I sat down at the mother machine. It looked just like the one I had been using. I went through the list of procedures I always followed, and waited. It started to work—then *blip,* it locked up and I could get no further.

I had no idea what should be done, but I did remember one move I had seen Alger make.

He's so busy, I'll just try it. Hey, if it doesn't work, he can just get me started again when he has a minute.

I pushed the mystery key in the upper right-hand corner. Suddenly there was dead silence in the room. No one moved for a moment. Only little gasps could be heard as everyone took in the gravity of the situation.

I looked as far to the left as I could without turning my head. If I moved, everyone in the room might realize that it was me who just lost half a morning's work for them.

I sensed Alger approaching quietly behind my back. I closed my eyes and braced for the rebuke.

"Hmm, let's see." Still calm and cool, he was trying to figure out what I had done. "Did you by any chance push this key up here?"

"What, me? Well, I may have, I guess. Er . . . yes." I tried to disappear through the bottom of the chair.

"You know, it's not a good idea to push that key." He was still sweet and polite. "That key shuts down the whole network, and you can see we have two printers and five typists running off this system. If you have a problem and you don't know what to do, just wait and I'll come and help."

"O.K.," I squeaked.

Needless to say, when personal computers became available I was one of the first to buy. I made sure it came with lots of nice, thick manuals and I spent hours sorting out my own problems. But I never messed up any-body else again.

I did make several trips to the computer department for advice, though. Sometimes the manuals forgot to tell you such steps as *push enter.* I needed all the help I could get.

There were other difficulties to be found when using computers. These were called "bugs," and I had a particular talent for finding them in programs that no one else thought possible.

My most remarkable find was the bug that caused the well-tested software created by Wycliffe programmers to "eat itself." The technician said quite frankly, when I described the problem, "That isn't possible. It can't happen." Then I demonstrated and, sure enough, it did.

Yes, there was always a bug somewhere.

My personal bugs were the jobs that seemed impossible ever to do correctly or completely—like treating some medical patients without a knowledge of what was really wrong with them; cleaning a village house that was dirty again almost before I finished scrubbing; producing literature in the Folopa language only to find mistakes the first time the book was opened, teaching school lessons to kids with a different agenda; learning about and obtaining sophisticated computer systems that became obsolete the month after I purchased them.

I always experienced forward motion but never the feeling of reaching a goal successfully. My petty troubles were not worth reporting in our quarterly newsletter, but they managed to consume my energy and leave me tired and defeated at the end of the day.

Lord, help me to do it right, I prayed.

But it always felt as if it was not right. And, looking at my track record, I wondered if I had been mistaken thinking I could serve God at all.

Attempting the Impossible

Troubles without number surround me; my sins have overtaken me, and I cannot see. They are more than the hairs of my head, and my heart fails within me.

Psalm 40:12

After four and a half years of moving every few months between the village and the Ukarumpa center, it was time to move to the U.S. for a year, starting in August 1976.

"It's so good to have you home," a gray-haired widow said at church the very first Sunday. "Isn't it wonderful you can have a year-long vacation? That should be plenty of time to get rested up for your next term on the field."

Furlough, though not a vacation, was a good break from the stresses and strains of missionary life. The five of us lived in a small rented house in Spokane owned by a couple in our church. The money we saved from the low rent allowed us to purchase needed equipment and clothing to take back when we returned the next year. In spite of all my worrying about how we would manage, it all worked out beautifully.

One of my desires for furlough was to explain as effectively as I could what life was like for us in Papua New Guinea. People could understand lifestyle hardships like doing without running water or electricity or a toilet. What was difficult to communicate were the personal and spiritual hardships we experienced. Was it O.K. to talk about being homesick or sometimes not wanting to return to the village because it was hard to face packing or to interact with people who were poor and sick when I was healthy and well fed? Could I tell about the real problems and still assure the people at home that the mission was being carried out—that we were doing our best to bring God's Word to a people group that, until we came, did not have a written language?

Speaking at a ladies' luncheon that fall, I gave it my best shot. I told of the medical successes and failures and of sounding like a two-year-old when I spoke the language. I shared about the young church with only the book of Genesis translated for them as yet, and how they did not understand God's gracious gift of His Son. They had been freed from the punishment for their sins and did not have to do good works to merit salvation.

"It's very difficult work," I said as I concluded my remarks. "Sometimes I think it's impossible work, but somehow we're going ahead with it. Please pray for us and remember each of the struggles I've mentioned."

The chairperson of the Women's Missionary Fellowship was asked to close in prayer.

"Lord, we thank You for the help You give the missionaries," she prayed. "You have made them extra special. Thank You for giving them such a large portion of Your grace that they don't have the worries and cares we do here at home."

I sat at the table dumbfounded. *Wait a minute! Didn't I just spend the last half-hour describing all the trials of missionary life? Why do you think missionaries have more grace available than the average person?*

By the time I had spoken at a few more functions, I understood for the first time the meaning of the "missionary pedestal" syndrome. Some people, it appeared, assumed that because Neil and I had spent four years mingling with "jungle natives," we were now higher and more spiritual than "ordinary" Christians. It seemed impossible to convince them otherwise.

In truth, our friends and family could not fully comprehend what we had been experiencing. It was foolish of me to think I could make them understand completely. They simply had not been where we had. But was I mistaken in talking about my real experience?

Neil and I spent the year loading up the borrowed car with a slide projector, a table display and our three children and traveling to a different church each Sunday.

"I guess the Lord never called me to be a missionary," I kept hearing over and over as we shook hands with parishioners after a service. "I'm terrified of spiders."

It was comforting to know that so many of my kind had similar fears. But it was hard to resist the temptation to come back with "Oh, I'm sorry to hear that. Missionaries have to pass a spider test before being sent overseas." After living four years in a rain forest, I was developing an attitude.

We came, spoke, showed slides, answered questions and drove home, exhausted.

"Mommy, why do we have to go to a different church every week? Can't we stay at the one where my friend Susie goes?" whined a tired daughter from the back seat.

"Which church was that one, Heather?"

"I don't know. The one with the red curtains, I think."

"I don't want to go to any more churches!" chimed in Danny from the other side of the back seat.

"Why not?" I asked.

"All those people keep staring at me," he sulked. "I don't want to say hi or shake hands. I just want to go play."

What could I say? It was ten churches down and seven to go before the end of furlough.

After seven or eight months we had done most of the things we had wanted to do, and we were looking forward to our return. It had been wonderful to be home, but the part of the body we had filled had been filled by others now. Our friends had closed the space in the circle we had left years before. Waves of time were washing away our roots. When the year was up, we were all happy to go back to the place our children now called home.

Our final week was spent in Portland, Oregon, attending a Christian living seminar along with thousands of other believers. After the final message on Saturday night, when the speaker gave a stirring challenge, I took the opportunity to pray and rededicate my efforts to the Lord for the coming term of service.

The first four years in Papua New Guinea had been difficult. There had been many adjustments to make and stresses to weather. Perhaps we had seen the worst of these, however, and could put it all behind us. Something new was about to begin and I wanted to start off on the right foot. Thinking of the many areas in which I felt I had failed, I prayed that the Lord would bless the new term with progress and success. The next time we came home, I would report that I had learned to speak the language well enough to be more of a help in the translation work. There were so many needs; the possibilities for service were unlimited.

It was our last day of furlough and I spent it lying in bed sick to my stomach.

Lots of people can wake up in the morning, be sick to their stomachs and think nothing of it. Not me. When

I do it, it means I can expect to wake up the next morning, too, sick to my stomach. In fact, nausea will be part of my life for the next eight months.

So on that Sunday morning, I assumed I would spend much of the next four to six months bent over the toilet (or the receptacle of my choice).

But still I felt defeated by this new turn in the road. I had been given a job that was very hard, and just when I sought to renew my efforts and hope for success, my life suddenly got more difficult and complex. How could I hope to accomplish my lofty goals now? Had I done something wrong and let God down somehow? How would His work ever get accomplished?

Wendy was born eight months into our new term. Four children were harder to handle, but there were still opportunities and quite a bit of time before our next furlough came around.

From this point on, when we went to the village, Heather would be staying at a children's hostel at Ukarumpa when school was in session.

When our new daughter was six months old, I started to cough. I coughed and hacked for six months and was tired and weak. After I had given up on regular antibiotics, I went to Lae for a tuberculosis test and chest x-ray.

Looking at the film, the doctor said, "Oh, just viral pneumonia. You'll get over it in time. From the looks of the scars on your lungs, I'd say you're almost clear."

It felt like six more months of uselessness added to my first eight back in the country.

Shortly afterward the whole family took turns having hepatitis. First nine-year-old Dan had it and was cleared of the disease in a month. Six weeks later we left Ukarumpa and our older daughter, and went out to Fukutao village, hoping we were past the point of incubation.

For Easter thirteen-year-old Heather, who had just finished her first term in middle school, rejoined the family for the two-week break. No sooner had she settled in than she began to vomit and could hardly get out of bed.

I came down with a fever and terrible pain under my ribs about the same time. Just when the fever let up, I vomited for days. Perhaps flu and malaria had struck, I thought, since it had been two months since Dan's sickness.

Heather and I were sitting up on the couch one afternoon after a week in bed. As we looked into each other's eyes, I noticed something. "Heather, your eyes are turning yellow."

No sooner had I said this than she shot back, "Hey, Mom, your eyes look yellow, too."

I thought she was joking, but without another word we both got up and staggered down the hall to look into the bathroom mirror. Hepatital eyeballs stared back at us.

That ended our stay in the village for quite a while. We were flown back to Ukarumpa the next day.

Less than a week later, we were not even settled into our home at Ukarumpa when Neil crashed onto the bed and said weakly, "I feel so sick."

"Oh, no, you don't," I protested. "This is my sickness and you can't have it. So get that out of your head right now."

Everyone in the family was relying on Neil to run the household. And besides, I was getting to like being waited on. In fact, after the first week of dire misery, hepatitis was not all that bad. It was like having enforced leisure with no guilt.

After five weeks I was back on top once again. Neil, sorry to say, went on being miserable for six months. He was such an active person normally that lying flat on his back for all those months itching (that was the part nobody told us about!) was almost more than he could bear.

The day finally came, however, when health had returned to all of us. Getting our strength back took some extra rest and patience, but we were finally ready to hop onto the helicopter and go back to work. More than half of our second term was behind us. Now where were those goals of mine?

One week after moving back to Fukutao in November, I was up to my usual activities—cleaning spider webs and cockroach droppings, emptying boxes, arranging shelves of schoolbooks and groceries, taking the kids through school lessons.

As I made the bed that morning, I noticed I had a sore throat and swollen glands. Come to think of it, I was tired, too.

Oh, just another of the zillions of kinds of flu available to catch from the neighbors, I thought, dismissing the symptoms. As a busy mother I seldom slowed significantly for colds or the flu.

Days passed. I expected any time to be getting better.

Days turned to months. I was dragging myself around the house barely able to cope.

After we returned to Ukarumpa in January, I went to the clinic. The nurse was not terribly impressed.

"You've been working too hard," she said. "Take a few days off and get some rest."

With four children one did not take a few days off and rest very easily. I returned to our house and continued in the drudgery day after weary day.

What I suspected was some kind of fatigue syndrome. During the years we had been in Papua New Guinea, I had seen a number of people, particularly women, suffer from long bouts of fatigue, sometimes lasting years. I shuddered to think this could happen to me.

So I prayed short, desperate prayers, along the lines of *Lord, help!* Even those prayers felt as if they were dropping to the floor with a thud moments after leaving my lips. I could imagine black clouds looming somewhere just over my head. Life became a pit that I could not crawl out of. What had happened to me? This kind of existence, barely hanging on from day to day, was the ultimate failure. I longed for each day to end so that sleep might swallow up my misery. But lying in bed hour after hour waiting for sleep to come was worse.

Months passed as I tried to go on with my normal activities. It only got colder and darker in my soul.

This job is impossible, I thought. *My life is impossible.*

One night during our last stay in the village before our second furlough, I got up quietly, trying not to awaken anyone. Something had to change, and prayer must be the answer.

I got down on my knees out in the living room and tried to communicate with God. There was not much to say that I had not said many times before. But over and over I prayed for healing and waited for some sign that God had heard.

The silence was deadly. There was nothing from on high, no sudden light illuminating the room, no flow of warmth. Only darkness and a feeling of being alone with no one to help.

Mosquitoes started buzzing in my ear—a sign that it was time to head back to the protection of the net. I decided there would be no miracles this night, and trudged back to bed.

It Will Never Happen to Me

"How I long for the months gone by, for the days when God watched over me, when his lamp shone upon my head and by his light I walked through darkness!"

Job 29:2–3

As the driver backed the Aviation Department van out of our driveway with Neil and me and our four children, I looked back at our Ukarumpa house. Sadness filled my heart because something inside said I would never come back again. I knew I was going to die.

The scene played in my imagination. I would be in the doctor's office. He would enter the examining room and announce soberly that I had three months to live. He would advise me to make my peace with the world. I would plan my funeral.

Goodbye, I whispered for the last time as we drove on down the road and left for our second furlough. It was May 1981.

Back in Spokane once again, I joined friends and family but felt utterly alone and defeated. Being with people became painful and awkward, so I avoided going to meetings. Fortunately my children were struggling with the idea of making the rounds to the seventeen churches again, so it worked out well for all concerned that Neil do the speaking and I stay home. I was relieved that I did not have to face those faithful people who had been supporting us all this time. I could try to put a smile face on it, but surely they would see through to the inside— that I was a failure as a missionary.

"Carol, the tests have all come back and I can't really find anything wrong with you," the doctor said, looking puzzled. "Your glands are swollen slightly but I find no infection. Are there any other symptoms you can think of that you haven't mentioned?"

I did a mental survey from head to toe.

"Well, there's this little pain about here," I said, pointing to the area around my lower abdomen.

I did not really want to have a serious condition, but I was sure there must be a physical reason for my suffering.

"We'll check it out." The doctor turned to order more tests.

With this batch I was now referred to a gynecologist. When the results were in, it was decided that the problems might be associated with some parts of my anatomy that I could get along without. So after a hysterectomy and five days in the hospital, I was sent home to mend.

One month later I checked in to see the doctor for what was supposed to be the last time.

"Well, I'll bet you're feeling better, right?" the nurse asked, confident of a positive response.

I shrugged, not knowing what to say. Parts of me did feel better, and I did not want to disappoint her. But the fact was, I wanted to crawl into a hole and die. How could I explain the black cloud that hovered over my head? No one else but me, apparently, could even see it.

"Physically I *am* feeling better," I reported as the nurse smiled cheerily. "But I'm still quite depressed."

Her face fell.

I knew they had been hoping for a happy ending for my case. Instead I found myself letting them down, letting everyone down. And admitting . . . admitting what? What I had heard myself say was, "I'm still quite depressed."

Did I really say that?

The nurse had slipped out momentarily and was just returning.

"The doctor will see you in his study," she said sympathetically, and led the way down the hall.

I followed timidly, feeling that I was being led to the courtroom for my sentencing after being found guilty. Oh, why had I said those words?

He looked concerned, sitting there behind his large desk. "What's this I hear about your feeling depressed?"

"That's right, doctor. I *am* depressed."

What was I saying? Such words had not passed my lips in all these many months. A specter was haunting me. It spoke from the black cloud, pointed a bony finger and demanded, *Weren't you the one who said, "Nothing like that will ever happen to me"?*

I winced and waited for the words of condemnation to come out of the doctor's mouth. Instead he said, "What you need is a shot of hormones."

I relaxed. Shots were no fun but I was off the dock for the time being. What a close call!

That was it from the medical profession. No more suggestions. When the last paper was processed, I felt as if I were left hanging out on a limb, and it was a long way to the ground. I had to hang on. The medical side of things offered no hope. But there was one new factor in my case. I began to see that there was the slightest chance that the problem was not physical.

It was November. The weather was getting colder and winter was coming. The children were excited because they had not seen snow for almost five years. Everyone was praying for a huge storm that would block the roads and close the school. So the kids were planning what they would do with their special day.

Neil and I had plans, too. Every month our calendar was dark with scribbles and memos. Just looking at all the handwritten appointments on every day tired me out. But some colleagues had made us promise before we left Papua New Guinea that we would attend a particular marriage conference that they had attended on their furlough. I was now looking at those squares on the calendar and thinking how much I wished I could get out of it.

I remembered the last big conference we had attended at the end of our first furlough, and the commitment I had made to give the Lord my best efforts for His work in the coming four years. Looking back now, I realized that the best I could do just did not amount to much. Nor did the thought of going to a marriage seminar appeal to me. Surely I did not need to be made aware of my failings in marriage as well as in my spiritual life and ministry. If only I were not so tired. Our friends would understand if I backed out, wouldn't they?

But Neil was giddy with excitement just thinking about the trip. He could not understand my reluctance. Because it took too much energy to push for any further action on the matter, I let it drop.

The day we left to drive to Portland for the Christian Marriage Encounter, I felt as though I were about to face an inquisition. In my mind I could see an encircling crowd of Carol's character flaws all pointing accusing fingers in my direction. I fought the panic.

About twenty couples, along with the seminar staff, gathered in the hotel conference center in Portland. As I sat in the conference room, I tried my best to look like a normal person, not to let any of the hysteria show. I was sure everyone thought I was a mental patient who had been let out on a pass.

"The emphasis of this weekend," the first speaker informed us, "will be on allowing each other as married partners to express our own feelings. If people are allowed to share honestly what they are feeling, then greater intimacy will grow. Feelings are neither good nor bad; they just are."

Trying not to make any squirmy moves lest they know I was uncomfortable, I kept thinking that the man speaking must have known I was coming. Someone had warned him, called ahead and said, "There will be this missionary woman in the audience who is about to flip out. Nail her. She's the one we want!"

I kept listening as we seminar participants were given our first assignment. We were to go to our private hotel rooms with our spouses and answer this question: "What does your emotional life look like? If you could come up with a picture, a mental image, what form would your feelings take?" We were to write the answer on paper individually, then come together as a couple and read to each other what we had written.

Later in our room, after completing the assignment, Neil and I prepared to share our answers.

"You go first," I said to Neil, curious as to how he would respond.

He launched into vivid descriptions of flowers and trees and blue skies. I could tell he was enjoying the exercise.

"Now your turn." He was all smiles and expectancy and leaned forward to hear my answer.

This had not been a difficult exercise. I had merely closed my eyes and instantly seen a picture in my head. It was very clear though somewhat alarming.

"I saw an enormous cube of ice, like a three-story building," I said, trying to sound matter-of-fact and controlled. "It's like dry ice and has vapors flowing from it. It's very cold."

Neil's face immediately registered shock.

"You never told me this before," he said, looking intently into my eyes as if to see something that had evaded his understanding.

"I never knew it before today. No one ever asked me this question."

"Why do you think your feelings are like a big ice cube?" he asked in bewilderment.

"Maybe because I've believed that feelings were somehow wrong. You know, if you feel bad, you probably have sin in your life. That kind of thing."

"What kind of feelings do you have?" Neil asked.

It was evident that there were areas we had not spent much time discussing.

"I'm not sure," was my reply.

It was true, I did not know what my feelings were. I just knew they were bad and that I did not want to have to face them. I wanted to believe they could be ignored, and perhaps they would cooperate and disappear. Wasn't that the spiritual thing to do? How many times had I heard Christian teachers say, "Don't rely on your feelings"? I was only trying to do what was right.

But the more Neil and I talked, the more we realized that by ignoring my negative thoughts and feelings, I had created a cold storehouse of hopelessness and despair in my life.

What were these destructive feelings, anyway? I remembered the harshness of a broken home, my fear of growing up, the many times as a youngster that I did not want to listen to the teasing taunts of others. More recently I had suffered overwhelming feelings of failure as a missionary. I could not understand why we had experienced so many setbacks, and now I feared that God had run out of patience with me.

Toward the end of the program, the speaker asked us to look once again at the image of our emotional lives. I saw the same huge ice block, but there was a change. The vapor was gone and the surface had a shiny look, as if it were warmer. Maybe admitting there was a problem and talking about it had made a difference.

The weekend finally ended. I was exhausted. What was I supposed to do with all this? Who would understand and help me sort through the mess I had made of my life? I did not know.

I guess I'll have to figure this out by myself, I thought.

Ask, Seek, Knock

I cry to you, O LORD; I say, "You are my refuge, my portion in the land of the living." Listen to my cry, for I am in desperate need.

Psalm 142:5–6

Record-breaking snow fell the next month. Heather and Dan were ecstatic when school was canceled and the road in front of our house was impassable. All four kids piled up snow in front of the garage and slid off the roof into the fluffy white stuff.

Watching my children through the kitchen window, I was glad they were enjoying the cold weather. The winter in my soul was not quite so much fun. My ice-block heart was searching for a way out of the cold. What had I done to make myself so miserable? There was something I was supposed to learn if only I could find out what it was.

As a young Christian, when I had called out to God for help, He had met me in real and tangible ways—sometimes with a verse of Scripture, sometimes with a sensation of His warm presence. Could it be that the kind of help I needed now required something more of me?

"Ask and it will be given to you; seek and you will find;
knock and the door will be opened to you."

Matthew 7:7

Jesus said these words and added,

"For everyone who asks receives; he who seeks finds;
and to him who knocks, the door will be opened."

verse 8

What should I search for? I asked myself. *What is it
that I need?*

> If you call out for insight
>   and cry aloud for understanding,
> and if you look for it as for silver
>   and search for it as for hidden treasure,
> then you will understand the fear of the LORD
>   and find the knowledge of God.

Proverbs 2:3–5

All the promises of God seemed to point me, on that
snowy afternoon, in the direction of searching for answers. I needed to understand where I went wrong.

"O Lord, I cry out to you for insight and understanding. I can't do this alone. You are the Great Healer, and
I've been asking for You to heal me for months. You have
answered because at least I'm beginning to see where I
am. Now You have to help me find the cause. How did
I get this way and how can I find my way back to where
I should be?"

As I continued to watch my four children playing, I
thanked the Lord that they were healthy and happy. Life
was not that bad. I was a Christian, I had a loving husband and we had a meaningful career serving in a place
where we were badly needed. Life was difficult, yes, but
still there were no outstanding traumas or troubles.

I closed my eyes and went back to a scene—a young

girl playing in the snow. Another child gave her a shove and over she went. The small face wrinkled up in pain and cries of protest and offense. *Don't cry. Don't let them see me cry. They'll know they've hurt me. I don't want anyone to know. How can I stop? I'll think about something else.*

I sat down with a cup of tea. *This is what I've done all my life,* I realized. It was the Lamaze method of emotion control. Willing myself to turn my attention away from the pain, I felt I could pretend it was not there. That had always seemed the best way to cope with the distresses of life.

But my method was backfiring now as forgotten miseries were coming back to haunt me.

Crash! I was awakened by noises that were no longer strange to me. It was happening again. *Bang!* I froze with terror, straining for the next sound. Yelling. A muffled scream. Then all was silent. I tried not to think about the meaning of what I had heard as I attempted to go back to sleep.

"Mommy, why are you crying?" I asked.

"Your father has a sickness; he drinks too much. Now he's gone and he's never coming back." Mother was sobbing.

Never coming back? Did I do something wrong?

I bit my lip and walked away.

"Carol, your grandmother is dead. She died in her sleep last night. The noise in the house was just too much for her. She couldn't stand all the commotion of taking care of you children."

My father reported these facts to my two brothers and me as we sat in the back seat of the car. He had said he was taking us out for ice cream, but really it was to tell us that, after our extended visit to our grandparents' home in California, we were being sent back home to Spokane.

We had killed our grandmother.

"Carol! Where are you?"

I was silent in my upstairs bedroom in the creaky old house, hoping to be left alone.

The footfalls faded and I was safe, back in the long, narrow closet—my special hiding place. Daydreams of a world without rejection, abandonment, anger and fear were much more pleasant than facing cold reality.

It was not hard to guess, without too much searching, how I had learned to shove my darker thoughts and feelings into a closet. It was my own personal storeroom where no one else could go. In this room, which had now turned into a cold storage locker, I began to realize there were rules for survival: *Don't acknowledge pain. Look the other way. Don't admit to anyone that it hurts. Anger will only get you in trouble, so don't ever let anyone see it.*

If others did not see the pain or anger, they would ask no questions—because, of course, it followed that there were no answers.

But there are answers, I reasoned as I sat analyzing my predicament. Surely the Bible had truth to teach about the inevitable pain of living in this world. And the prime source of pain was not physical but emotional, stemming from relationships with people.

Perhaps some of the misery resulted from my responses toward those who had hurt me: my father, who had abandoned our family, leaving us to wonder if we had done something wrong to make him go; my grandfather, who had lashed out and blamed me for my grandmother's death; my stepfather, who hardly ever spoke to me. The list went on and on of people I chose to blame for my perceived problems.

But all that was now in the past. So why had I carefully stored all the pain, reserving the right to go into the cold storage locker and review the contents periodically? Why did I keep those hated memories like corpses in a morgue?

I had attended seminars, heard sermons and read books and lots of Scripture on forgiveness. I had gone through the motions and said the words, but had never realized until this moment, now that my life had gone haywire, that I had not completed the process.

Rereading the Scriptures I knew about forgiveness, I was reminded by Jesus that "if you forgive men when they sin against you, your heavenly Father will also forgive you. But if you do not forgive men their sins, your Father will not forgive your sins" (Matthew 6:14–15).

"Lord, I've kept these putrid dead bodies of anger and hatred for so long. They have smelled up my life, and I think they're killing me. I've got to unload this junk. Help me throw the whole mess out once and for all."

The last step was to let go of the anger and hatred. It did not happen overnight. But the Lord heard my request for help. He helped me see that I had brought into my Christian life, starting way back when I was thirteen, quite a bit of baggage, in the form of memories, habits and ways of thinking. One by one, as situations came to mind, I gave them to the Lord and asked Him to take them away forever.

The black clouds began to lift. The tiredness and hopelessness faded as I turned away from the dark specter of unforgiveness.

In the months that followed, I experienced relief from most of my symptoms. But I still had a vague emptiness. It was spring again, but early spring, before the green leaves had fully budded on the trees. It had been almost two years since I started feeling tired and depressed—our last year in Papua New Guinea and then most of our furlough year. Now, it seemed, the worst was over. Perhaps in time the flatness, too, would grow into something more lifelike.

Before I knew it the six of us were back in Papua New Guinea for our third term—the place to which I thought I would never return alive. We would once again plan, pack, clean, move, resettle and unpack, first at the center, Ukarumpa, and then in Fukutao village.

ꕤ   ꕤ

The door creaked on its hinges as it swung open. We peered into the dim interior of our village house, taking immediate note that there was no major damage. It had been more than a year since we had been here, giving the rats, spiders and cockroaches plenty of time to make themselves at home. The usual pile of cardboard boxes waited on the front porch, having been carried from the helicopter by a troop of young Folopa boys. We had shaken hundreds of hands, smiled and said *koneo* until our mouth muscles drooped.

"Seven women and two men have died while you were away," Naniae's father reported as he shook our hands.

A small figure pushed his way to the front of the crowd and looked up at me sadly. It was Apusi, my son Bruce's playmate.

"My mother is dead," he declared mournfully and waited for my reaction.

Apusi's mother had been in poor health for years, but it was a shock to realize she was gone.

"I'm very sorry," I said, trying to show the concern and sadness I felt.

The problem was, there was too much to feel in those first moments back in the village. All the news, good and bad, was delivered in the first few minutes, and already I was drained of energy responding to it.

"The water isn't coming," I yelled to Neil, who was surveying his workroom.

This was not welcome news either, for it meant a hike to the source of the spring water pipe fifteen minutes' walk from the house, and some sloshing in mud and leeches until it was unplugged and running freely once again.

"I can't fix that until I see if the generator is working," he yelled back.

"I want a drink of water," said Wendy.

"Can we start school now?" asked Bruce.

I've heard this before, I thought.

Some things never changed. Even though our older children, Dan and Heather, were at Ukarumpa attending high school, we relived some of the same scenes from the past through Bruce and Wendy, years younger.

I heard a *hmmm* throat-clearing sound at the door. Reluctantly I turned to answer it, purposing to go and do what I could.

"Heto Hama, I just came from the garden and haven't shaken your hand yet."

It was Hariso Hama, looking a bit thinner but as jolly as ever. I shook her hand and looked around at the other faces. Each stared at me as if waiting for just the right moment to present his or her needs.

The familiar feeling of dread swept over me. Why should I feel this way? I had only just gotten back and was ready to run away and hide. It was not any one factor but the sum of all the needs that surrounded me—needs I could hardly begin to meet—that affected me. There was no medicine for the ailments at my door like chronic lung disease, cancer and crippling arthritis. I had little with which to comfort young Apusi for the death of his mother, not to mention all the others who had lost loved ones in recent months.

But they all continued to stand and wait while I continued to unpack and clean the house. To stop and talk meant finding out more about their tragic lives. I could not bear the thought of knowing more than I already did.

What else can I do? I've let them down. I've disappointed God. Why does the Lord even bring me back here when all I do is let Him down?

I had thought that when I confessed to God the hidden unforgiveness in my heart, I would become a more mature and loving Christian. But something important was missing. And I did not feel I could even face the Lord with all my weaknesses and failures.

⚭   ⚭

The following Sunday afternoon I sat down with David Needham's book *Birthright* (Multnomah, 1979). A friend had given it to us before we left and had highly recommended it.

This will never work, I thought. Whenever I opened a book, a signal went off in the atmosphere reminding my kids that it was time to ask me for something.

I plunged into the book anyway, part of me waiting in my mental reception room for the first call for "Mom!"

Silence.

After reading for a while, absorbing the new ideas, I was captured by a chapter title: "Where Is the Joy?"

Yes! I said to myself. *I want to know. Joy is the issue now.*

There had been no joy in my life for a long time.

I continued to read, when tears began to flood my eyes. I suddenly realized where I had gone wrong. The Lord had long been telling me that He loved me. Now I realized that I had not believed it. I had reasoned to myself that others were loved, not me. I was not worth loving and forgiving, so it could not be true.

The message was finally getting through. According to this author, if I believed that God loved and accepted me as His chosen, adopted and totally forgiven child, that would be cause for real joy.

The process had begun, I knew, with my forgiving others. Now forgiveness had to be taken a step further by my accepting God's forgiveness of my sins: "There is now no condemnation for those who are in Christ Jesus" (Romans 8:1). If I could believe I was totally forgiven, perhaps I could believe in God's great love for me as well.

As I sat and meditated on this, I realized that I carried all the information, like the concept of forgiveness, already in my head. Not believing it to be true did not make it false; it only meant I had nothing about which to rejoice. Joy, I could now see, was a result of believing and fully accepting these truths.

In my Christian experience, I had to admit, I had seen God as a moderately patient and forgiving Father. But behind His back I knew He was hiding a big club. He was just waiting, and one day He would run out of patience with all my failures and weaknesses and bring the club down on my head. Never did I imagine God smiling at me with warm acceptance and love. If He ever spoke to me from heaven, I thought He would say, "Not again, Carol! Good grief, where did I get this child?"

Look at me! I thought. *Haven't I dedicated my life to translating a Book that I believe to be God's revelation to mankind and the only source of authoritative truth? Am I so busy giving it to others that I forgot it's true for me as well?*

What did that Book say God is like?

> He tends his flock like a shepherd:
>   He gathers the lambs in his arms
> and carries them close to his heart;
>   he gently leads those that have young.
>   Isaiah 40:11

> The LORD is righteous in all his ways
>   and loving toward all he has made.
> The LORD is near to all who call on him,
>   to all who call on him in truth.

> He fulfills the desires of those who fear him;
> he hears their cry and saves them.
> The LORD watches over all who love him. . . .
>
> Psalm 145:17–20

And, most familiar of all,

> For God so loved the world that he gave his one and
> only Son. . . .
>
> John 3:16

My concept of God had been greatly distorted. I could see that. But could He really love me? And could I accept this as a hard fact?

"God, do You really love me?" I asked, thinking what a dumb thing that was to ask God.

My mind immediately went back to the night I had asked God, after my drug reaction and gangrene, why I had to suffer through that painful illness.

The answer had not changed. It was still *I love you.*

Would I believe it at last, even though I could not see why He would love me?

"God, I've been wrong. You *are* a loving Father who gently leads those who are feeble and weak. I want to believe You love me every day of the week, even when I fail. Lord, I do believe in Your love, which was so great You sent Your Son to suffer and die for me."

Believing all over again in the simple Gospel message seemed like a small step to take, but the result was vastly significant. The joy I had missed for a long time came flooding back. God was, after all, a merciful and loving Father. He was there for me when I needed Him.

It had taken emotional pain and suffering for me to realize I was depressed. That pain did not go away until the Lord taught me some vitally important lessons. If I had been simply healed of my depression when I had prayed for relief, I would have missed the most important part. There was a cleansing and teaching purpose for it all.

In the weeks that followed, I read great portions of the Bible as if for the first time. How had I missed all those verses that assured me of God's love and acceptance? I had not missed reading them; I had only failed to believe them. The door of truth had been standing open, but I had not knocked very hard before now.

How I regretted that much of my suffering had come from my own ignorance and refusal to accept what had been given to me! In receiving it now, I was giving myself the joy of focusing on the most important truth in the world—God's unconditional love.

The Worth of a Woman

He lifted me out of the slimy pit, out of the mud and mire; he set my feet on a rock and gave me a firm place to stand.

Psalm 40:2

Feet shuffling on palm boards and a coughing sound came from the front porch, confirming that a visitor waited to speak to me.

"*Yae,*" I responded from where I stood at my kitchen counter kneading bread dough. ("Speak.")

"Bring the ghost-getting thing and come quickly," Naniae urged politely.

"Is it time? We'll be right there. Come on, kids, it's time to go see Kepawhiso get married."

I covered the bread dough with a cloth, washed the stickiness off my hands, got my camera and we all headed out the door.

The equatorial sun was intense, the sky blue and cloudless.

What a beautiful day! I thought. *But what a day to have to stand out in the open for hours.*

We walked through Fukutao's small grouping of houses, down the narrow path to the next hamlet on the ridge. There in Sapaaletao a large gathering of villagers milled about, waiting for the final stages of what had taken weeks to prepare.

The bride-to-be stood in the clearing in front of the men's house, hanging her bark-caped head dejectedly. Looking at her, one would never think this was the biggest day in her life. Dressed in her usual old cotton dress, she could have been on her way to work in the garden. In front of her on the ground, sheets of flattened tree bark lay covered with red cloth. The groom's clan were positioning items of wealth on the cloth that would make up the brideprice.

There were rows of crescent-shaped kina shells, plastic packages of salt, string bags and pieces of colored fabric. The final and most important touch was the blue-green and red paper currency of Papua New Guinea being placed painstakingly under each shell. Fussing over and caressing each bill, the clansmen carefully arranged and then rearranged the money in a pleasing pattern. Handing it all over to the other clan would not be easy.

"Five hundred kina," an older man shouted. "It is enough."

"How many pigs?" returned the brother of the bride.

"Ten big pigs," he snapped, and motioned for the pigs to be brought forward.

A team of family volunteers jumped into action, each leading a pig from behind the communal house. There were loud snortings and squealings as the blinded animals were swatted and prodded along toward the stake to which each would be tethered. The critical eyes of the bride's relatives went up and down the line.

"These are not big pigs," shouted a brother. "She's a good woman and worth more than this."

"What do you mean?" countered the prospective mother-in-law. "Look at her. She's so thin she'll probably die of sickness in no time. Look at those breasts. Her children will starve for lack of milk."

I listened to the proceedings, trying to follow the dialogue. Looking into the face of the bride, which was by now dripping with perspiration, I noted her unhappy appearance.

"Why is she sad?" I asked the bride's aunt.

"She's very happy," said the Folopa woman, surprised that I did not understand. "This is a big payment and she has been shown to be worth much."

When the final details were settled, I was summoned to record for history, and the photo album, the exact amount of Kepawhiso's worth in the bride market. After I photographed the small fortune, it was loaded carefully into a large string bag and hung from the bride's head and down her back. She then led the pigs, with the help of her sisters and mother, up the hill, walking slowly to the men's house where her father lived. The whole display would be laid out again later and divided among her extended family members.

This was not really a wedding. In fact, the Folopa people did not have weddings. It had been merely the final settlement of the price that the groom's clan would pay for the bride—a standard practice in Papua New Guinea. Once the bride's family accepted the payment, the marriage was virtually sealed. After this, Kepawhiso's family would reciprocate with similar items of wealth. There would be exchanges of hunted game and favors that would stretch the obligations out for years to come. But for now, Kepawhiso was officially married.

Sunburned and thirsty, Neil, Bruce, Wendy and I plodded up the hill and back home. I wondered as I walked along what it would be like to have one's worth up for public discussion. Was this young woman concerned about the evaluation of the community, or did she accept the whole proceeding as just another cultural ritual to get through so the marriage would become finalized?

Putting myself in her place, I imagined how I would feel. Much of my evaluation of myself came from how

I thought other people perceived me. Then there was God. What He thought of me now made a very big impact on what I thought of me.

My self-image and its relationship to the truth revealed in God's Word intrigued me to the point that I decided to list Scripture verses on the subject. The next morning I sat down with my Bible and opened to the letter from Paul to the Ephesians. I began to read the first chapter carefully. As believers we are:

Holy and blameless in His sight	verse 4
Adopted as His sons	verse 5
Adopted in accordance with His pleasure and will	verse 5
Freely given His grace	verse 6
Redeemed through His blood	verse 7
Forgiven of our sins	verse 7
Redeemed and forgiven through the riches of His grace	verse 7
Recipients of His grace lavished on us	verse 8
Made aware of the mystery of His will	verse 9
Made aware of His will according to His good pleasure	verse 9
Chosen and predestined	verse 11
For the praise of His glory	verse 12
Included in Christ	verse 13
Marked in Him with a seal	verse 13
Marked by the promised Holy Spirit	verse 13
God's possession to the praise of His glory	verse 14

My notes grew in length as I continued to read the first three chapters of Ephesians. After that point Paul began to exhort the believers to behave in a way consistent with the truth of the first chapters.

For the first time it occurred to me that the motivation for Christian behavior was not impressing people or even convincing God that I was worth having as His child. It was not about earning points to achieve some level of spirituality. It was about gratitude for being given a free and undeserved package deal—eternal life and more blessings than I could count!

When I was girl I joined a Girl Scout troop. Was it because I liked to attend meetings or go on field trips? No, the reason was, I wanted a uniform. I wore that green dress proudly to show I belonged to something important. I had an identity. Even more important to me was the sash that was worn over one shoulder, down across the chest and under the other arm. On this sash were sewn the numbers of the troop, the Girl Scout pins and the merit badges.

Oh, how I wanted those badges! I studied the manual hours on end, reading the requirements for each badge, until I found one I was capable of doing. When it was completed and awarded, I was on cloud nine. I felt like a worthwhile human being. I could wear my accomplishments—my worth—on my sash for all the world to see.

Now, in Fukutao, when I remembered those little pieces of cloth and how much importance I gave them, it seemed childish. But in different ways I had kept doing the same thing into my adult life. I had chosen the accomplishments—constructing a survival shelter at Jungle Camp, perhaps, or typing up neat pages of translation text from Genesis—and set the standard for the results. Then, all these years, I had been making a mental list of accomplishments, adding them to various pins and awards from high school and totaling them up to tell me that I counted for something.

When I was not able to accomplish what I had hoped, or if I did not meet the standard I had set, then a different feeling resulted—one of failure and worthlessness.

Nepiame's old aunt was one of those people who tried hard and failed. Once she had been young and pretty. She had paraded her wealth through the hamlet, proud to be marrying a proven warrior. But garden work, sickness and poor nutrition eventually took their toll. Then her two babies died, one after the other, leaving her childless. She never became pregnant again, year after year.

Her angry husband demanded to know why she was holding out on him. "Why are you not giving me children?"

There was nothing to say. She wanted children with all her heart.

"Woman, you must be working some magic to prevent your having a child. I will throw you away and you will be forever stood as a tree, barren and dead to me. I am binding another woman to take your place."

So the devastating pronouncement was made.

From then on she was a nobody. There was no polite name for her, not So-and-So's wife or So-and-So's mother. She became a "nothing" woman—the aunt who was not an aunt of her husband's future children by his new wife.

One day she died and no one mourned. She had tried just as hard as every other woman, but had failed.

As I read and reread the Bible passages in my notebook, I was relieved that in God's sight my worth was not based on what I had been able to achieve. Adding all the bits of cloth, pins and awards to my current accomplishments as a missionary revealed a sad picture. There was no way I could meet God's standard by trying hard. I would never be accepted on the basis of my achievements.

How eternally grateful I was that my worth was based on what Jesus did for me, on who I was in Him and not on anything I was expected to do.

I still desired greatly to do something with my life that was lasting and important. I still wanted to be successful and accomplish what I set out to do. But I learned that God was smiling at me. In fact, He was bursting with excitement when He saw that I liked the gifts He had given me. He was not holding a club behind His back waiting for the results of my work. Like a loving father, He was waiting for just the right moment to produce another beautifully wrapped gift.

When I focused on Jesus and all the benefits of knowing Him, my heart filled with joy. In my great pleasure, I found a strong desire to do His will.

How could I have been so wrong about God all those years? How had I read the Bible and not seen everything that Jesus Christ had done for me and how important each truth was? I had suffered for years thinking that my worth depended on my performance. My miseries were a direct result of ignorance. Now, each time I read the Scriptures, I found more and more to learn about the Lord. Every time I searched for some new truth about His character, I was rewarded. I was also learning that I was His special creation, given the gift of worth that I did not have to earn and did not have to maintain with a series of successes. All I had to do was obey His commands, and He promised to produce the fruit.

What other important things had I missed? Reading the apostle Paul's prayer, I decided to pray for myself the same words:

> I keep asking that the God of our Lord Jesus Christ, the glorious Father, may give [me] the Spirit of wisdom and revelation, so that [I] may know him better. . . . that the eyes of [my] heart may be enlightened in order that [I] may know the hope to which he has called [me], the riches of his glorious inheritance in the saints, and his incomparably great power for us who believe.
>
> Ephesians 1:17–19

Digging Up
Buried Treasure

"Everyone who has will be given more, and he will have an abundance."

Matthew 25:29

What's going on here?" I asked Neil as he came in the front door. A restless crowd was milling about in front of our porch and the mood was hostile.

We went outside and stood in the shade, wondering what was brewing in this normally peaceful setting.

"The village leaders of the community work project will be handing out the pay from the government," Neil replied.

The local government had allotted a lump sum of money to the village for labor on improvements to the trails surrounding Folopa land. Fukutao residents had very little education in math, so the equitable distribution of the funds was a great challenge.

"I don't think all the people understand the method of dividing the money," he added.

Mumbled threats and angry gestures could be heard and seen here and there across the crowd of some eighty people.

Suddenly all was quiet. Attention was riveted on the handful of men who stood on the top step of the small building next to our home, normally used for typing and preparing Folopa literacy materials. The village leaders had decided it was a good spot to make a speech and hand out portions of the government money each person had earned.

Our eyes darted from one person to another as sparks of tension crackled in the crowd.

Each leader gave a short speech explaining the method of dividing the pay. Then the money was passed out to the many who had worked, each getting a share.

But a sinister-looking young man leaning against a fence pulled himself forward, bent to pick up a stone and threw it straight at the speaker, narrowly missing him. That was all it took to spark the melee that followed. I expected that the worst would be over in a few minutes, but I was wrong.

Never had I witnessed anything like this. People were screaming at each other, some brandishing clubs and pieces of firewood that seemed to appear from nowhere. Some pushed and some pulled on one another. Large stones were hurled through the air, mainly toward the front of the literacy office. I winced each time one of them crashed through a window or broke another hole through the sago palm roof. The building was quickly becoming a wreck. The village leaders had taken cover inside but were still at risk (along with the typewriters and hand-crank duplicator) from stones coming through the leaf roof.

At this point it was best to look somewhere else. Our whole family contemplated going into the house just in case a stone came our way. But there seemed to be no danger of that; the mayhem was confined pretty well to the immediate area outside the office.

It was then I noticed that there was also a group of Folopa spectators—people who were not joining in the fight. Wondering why some were in it tooth and nail and others just sat and watched, I determined to see what I could see. And from this fracas I learned something important about the Body of Christ and what we contribute as individuals to our life together.

There were actually four roles that were played by people involved directly with the fight. And, to be more precise, what was happening before us was not really a fight but a demonstration. On previous occasions, when we had seen an angry crowd of people gathered to resolve a problem, a designated young male would make all the motions of attacking an opponent. At that point an older male relative held the aggressor back from doing any real harm. A third party was a female relative who also restrained in some way, and the fourth was another female who incited action, usually with inflammatory language. With all these roles functioning, the argument was aired, strong feelings were expressed and no one was hurt. We had seen it many times before—only not with this many people involved.

Now as I saw the jumble of people pulling and pushing each other, it began to make sense. A man was attempting to throw a stone, but his arm was being held back by another who stood close in behind him. A woman was lying on the ground with her arms around the aggressor's leg, and another woman was yelling at him to hurry up and throw. This scene was multiplied times twenty.

Around the edges of the arena was the group of spectators. Most were either too old or too young for this kind of activity. Some of the old men looked as if this was nothing new and merely waited, with a ho-hum kind of look on their faces, for it to be over. Some sports-commentator types were only too willing to give play-by-play observations and background information. Finally there were the mature, serious, wise leaders whose responsibility it would be to bring all these people together again and mediate for reconciliation.

It was hard for me to believe that the whole mess would be straightened out and that life would settle down and return to normal. There would be some wounds that needed doctoring and some damages that would require compensation. And despite the negative consequences, the angry hotheads would wait for the next opportunity to break loose. The peacemakers would be ready for them.

Sure enough, the next day a feast was held to bury the hatchet, so to speak. Everyone apologized and ate together happily. All the mean things that had been said and done seemed to be forgotten as, officially, the case was closed.

Thinking about this incident, and about the Folopa culture, always made me think about my own culture. How did we fight and make up again? Did we, too, have people who play distinct roles? Then I considered the Body of Christ and our often fitful attempts at community. What role did I play in keeping everything together? Did the Body grow or was it hurt by my contribution?

After returning to Papua New Guinea and coming to grips with God's love and forgiveness, I found the quality of my Bible reading changed. I read the Scriptures as if every word was important and deeply meaningful. Being accepted by God and sensing His grace was cause for the greatest joy I had ever experienced. It gave me a strong desire to be and do all that the Lord wanted.

Reading books about who I was in the Body of Christ fueled a curiosity in me to know more of my God-given potential. I knew Christians are not all the same. We are different, each with our own role to fulfill in the Church. Natural and spiritual gifts, as well as personal preferences, accounted for most of these differences.

My husband and I responded to a questionnaire about personality preferences and saw for the first time how similar we were in some areas. The shock came when we also realized how opposite we were in others. This, of course, was nothing new. But I began to realize that perhaps God had created Neil to be the way he was, and that it was up to me not only to appreciate the brilliant and gifted parts, but also the aspects that were frustratingly opposite to me. God had given us each other and it had been a package deal.

Neil was one relieved guy when I finally said to him, "You know, you don't like to buy the airline tickets for furlough until the week before we're to leave. I prefer doing that many months in advance. You like to go to events where you can talk to lots of people. I prefer smaller groups or individuals. Somehow I think I can accept this if you can."

I was finally letting him off the hook after spending more time than I cared to think about being angry and confused about why we always responded so differently to things.

As far as my own orientation, I had expected the questionnaire to show that I had a real bent for scrubbing floors or attacking mountains of laundry. If it had suggested that I give serious thought to running a daycare center or becoming a professional cook, I would have sent the test results straight out the window. Instead, to my surprise, it said that people with my preferences often employed them in the arts, even writing. I was not even aware that these were possibilities, tending to wonder if there were any missionary career opportunities in fumigation. Challenged as I was thinking about future options and untapped gifts, there was also the possibility that I was misusing what I had been given.

And what about spiritual gifts? If the Scripture teaches that each one of us has a spiritual gift for building up the Body of Christ, what was mine? I began to read up on the subject. One author suggested that I could identify my spiritual gift by recognizing the thing I loved to do most in the world and could not stop doing if I tried. What was the thing that came naturally to me—that I did, like these Folopa, without stopping to decide which role I would play?

After much thought I decided that I love to find out what makes things tick, why things are the way they are, and the meaning of what I found out. No doubt I would have been sitting on the sidelines of the fight watching and preparing to help sort out the quarrel in the end. I would be trying desperately to discern the cause so I could tell everyone afterward, and in this way prevent it from happening again.

The best I could come up with for me as part of the metaphorical Body of Christ was a nerve with a direct connection to the brain. And if I was some kind of nerve, how could God use that? Was this an indication of a spiritual gift such as knowledge, wisdom or discernment?

I did not know the answer but determined to keep on looking. That is when I read Matthew 25, the Parable of the Talents.

I was familiar with the story. A man went on a journey and planned to be away for a while. To his servants left behind he entrusted his property. To three different ones he gave a portion of his money, expecting them to use it wisely. Each received a different amount according to his ability. Two of the servants invested the money and gained a return, so that when the master came back and saw what they had done, he was very pleased with them. But the third servant, afraid he would blow the whole deal, chose to bury the money rather than risk losing the little he had. It would be hidden safely in the ground, he thought, where no one else could get it. But the master was not pleased with his decision and sent him away to suffer the dire consequences of wasting precious opportunities.

That lazy servant and I had something in common, I realized: fear. We were both afraid to take risks, afraid to fail, afraid to be laughed at or to look stupid. We had both decided to bury the most precious thing we had—the gift from the Master.

With the servant it had been a simple act of digging a hole in the ground, placing the money into it and covering it with dirt. With me it had been reluctance to believe I had much to offer the Body of Christ, and therefore not using whatever it was I had been given. Because I saw no outstanding abilities, I figured I must have been passed over when it came to gift distribution.

There were things I had wanted to do but did not, for fear that I would do them poorly. What opportunities would be open to me if I spoke the Folopa language better, or got more involved in the difficult work of translation? In the past I had played the role of bystander—at best, perhaps, picking up the trash after the fight. I knew there was more I could do, but I felt intimidated by others who were more gifted. Now I realized for the very first time that perhaps God was not as interested in my level of skill as I was!

Not only fear kept me from serving God fully and joyfully, but pride. Failure to perform up to my own high standards was painful and embarrassing. Why look for more pain when I could hardly stand the pain I had already? Better to be safe than sorry. It had indeed been pride that had kept me from saying yes to opportunities to serve.

It was time to dig up the buried treasure—time to stop expecting myself to be perfect and highly skilled, and time to serve the Lord with gratitude, thanking Him for the small ability I did have. It was time to give up self-pity, which resulted from feeling I was not as talented as I would like to be. With self-pity had come a private misery that, like the lump of clay, always asked the Potter, "Why did you make me like this?" (Romans 9:20).

I found another answer, too:

But God chose the foolish things of the world to shame the wise; God chose the weak things of the world to shame the strong. He chose the lowly things of this world and the despised things—and the things that are not—to nullify the things that are, so that no one may boast before him.

1 Corinthians 1:27–29

Now was the time to practice and use what I had been given, humble as it was, until it had grown and multiplied and I could return ten times as much to the Master when He returned to settle accounts. I longed to hear Him say, "Well done, good and faithful servant."

The View from Above

"Be still, and know that I am God; I will be exalted among the nations, I will be exalted in the earth."

Psalm 46:10

hump, thump, thump. The cadence of marching feet tramped out of the real world into the fog of dreamland. Slowly I awakened to the familiar sound of chanting male voices and the continuing slap of broad, bare feet on the split palm floor. Had the men really been at this all night? I squinted, trying to see through the mosquito net to look at the clock. 5:30 A.M.

No need for the alarm today, I sighed as I reached over to hit the button.

This was the third day of continuous practice up in the men's house for the *Foke.* Up and down the narrow center hallway they tramped in unison as the caller hoarsely sang out the verse. Replying as if in agreement, the warriors' *Ya! ya! ya!* slowly faded before a pause and the next call. I hated to think what the real thing would be like if this was just the rehearsal.

175

Everyone in the village seemed excited about the coming feast they called *Foke*. As far as Neil and I could tell, it was the only big occasion of its kind.

Hardly anyone could remember for sure when the last *Foke* had taken place. The oldest man in the village said it was before government patrols came regularly into the Folopa area. That would make it more than twenty years before, in the early 1960s.

"It's like your Christmas," said Hariso Hama, who as our nearest neighbor had seen our celebration of Christmas. "Everyone gives gifts to everyone else." She glowed with anticipation and excitement.

All kinds of gifts had to be given year-round for births, deaths and maintaining family peace and tranquillity. Everyone would kill a pig and share the meat around to fulfill their obligations, which were many. For every marriage there had to be gifts going both ways to the extended families. For every child gifts were required for the mother's brother and his children. Men from each clan married women from all the other twelve clans, so the process was complicated.

Even so, everyone knew exactly to whom he or she was indebted. Those who gave large or extra portions were well thought of in the community. *Generous* and *greedy* were two concepts well understood by the Folopa people. So *Foke* gave everybody an opportunity to square up on their social indebtedness.

We kept asking when *Foke* would actually take place, but no one could say for sure. Later we learned that it would come after the current crop of vegetables was harvested, when the garden season ended and during the period of time before the new gardens were planted, when little was required in the way of labor. It would be months before that time came, so there was plenty of time for preparation.

And prepare they did. The chanting and marching went on and on, casting an aura of dull exhaustion over the men, who now had little time for sleep.

Little had we known that we were partly responsible for this event. Pigs were the main dish at a feast, and killing pigs was a central event. We were told that unless there were a great number of pigs alive, there could be no *Foke*. It just happened that two years before, Neil and a visiting doctor had inoculated every swine they could find against anthrax, a common killer of pigs. Our desire had been to help make a better supply of protein available to the villagers. But instead of killing the pigs a few at a time for special meals, they were being saved for a feast, and now a record number were alive and kicking. In fact, the pig population was getting out of hand. High-pitched squeals punctuated the airwaves all hours of the day and night. The time to kill the pigs had definitely arrived.

We got the impression that because it had been so many years since there were enough pigs to have a *Foke*, people had forgotten how to prepare for the feast properly. This apparently was being remedied with training and disciplined drill. The sergeants of this informal army were the old men who had fought and killed enemies in battles of yesteryear. They alone remembered how to paint the body and decorate it with feathers, shells and fur. The older women looked on with pride as their sons and grandsons now learned the ancient skills.

In the dark of the men's house, they secretly painted each other's faces, placed the old fur- and feather-trimmed headpieces on heads, wrapped their chests in ancient bark belts covered with tiny shells, pulled on more recently woven leg and armbands and hung pig tusk necklaces around their necks. With ax in one hand and bow and arrows in the other, the outfit was complete.

During the daytime hours the marching took place in the *be bela,* or open area in front of the men's communal house, called the *dape.* From inside the *dape* they came two by two, in a long line, their faces looking fiercely straight ahead. Fifty yards beyond the *dape* was the *temake be*—unusual as the only round building in the village. The marchers would circle around the *temake be,* then head back to the long, narrow building from which they had emerged.

"What is that round house, the *temake be?*" we had asked a number of times over the years since we had arrived to take up this work in the language group. We had hoped to get more clues as to its use, but until now no one had been willing to talk about it.

"In times past," we were told, "when men were injured in battle, they would recuperate in there, where no one could see their wounds or their shame at being weak and injured. Inside a man would grow strong again. If anyone was critically ill, he was laid in the *temake be* to be healed."

Another said, "During the feast the men would bury small stone carvings of yams and other garden vegetables in the dirt floor of the house. They would chant over the stones and then sleep on them, thereby making the gardens good."

Still another man had said, "The *dape* house is man and the *temake be* is woman."

This was very interesting, but what was the connection with all this information?

"What does that chanting mean?" we asked the old head man.

He looked as if that were too difficult a question to answer. "The words are about mountains, streams, animals, birds, the sky. But that is not what the chanting means. The words are hidden talk for other things. They are about fighting. . . ." He paused. "It's too hard to tell you."

It must have been like trying to explain Shakespeare to someone who barely knew English.

We asked others about the meaning of the *doware fo,* or chanting.

"You don't want to know that," they said. "The *doware fo* is not for Christians to think about. It's bad."

Now this was a mystery. Why did they not want to tell us what the words were?

I tried listening carefully, with no success. The voice quality of the caller made the words almost impossible to make out. Still, Neil and I continued to ask, even though it seemed as if we were getting nowhere.

Several weeks later the feast still had not happened. It was our scheduled time to leave the village and return to Ukarumpa. Sadly we left, only to find out a few days after our departure that the feast was finally taking place. It was very disappointing to miss the grand finale. When would there be another event like this one? We did not understand the full meaning behind this important episode in Fukutao village's life, and now it looked as if we would never find out.

Several years went by and the mystery was no closer to being solved. Since my children were getting older, my role had changed and I had more time to work directly with the language. I began to take over study of the grammar and dictionary from Neil so he would have more time to spend on translation.

Solving language problems turned out to be a challenging and enjoyable task. There were still a number of unsolved mysteries waiting for me to analyze, to make our understanding of the grammar more complete.

As I worked painstakingly on my latest problem, that of settling on a final form for the Folopa alphabet, I began to find some startling features that we had missed. Most of the verbs that began with the letter *d*, for instance, represented important activities—strong action producing significant results.

Interesting. Would it have any impact on our translation efforts?

I focused on some of the words that began with *d* to see how important they really were. The word *dowa* (grow) was a puzzle because it seemed to be one of the few verbs that did not have the impact of other words like *dae* (kill) or *diri* (to be hard).

Something clicked in my brain. *Doware fo* from the *Foke* feast meant something about growing—the *doware* (growth) *fo* (talk). Could it mean that the chanting from the feast preparations was about trying to get something to grow? And how important was it to do that? It was time to check this out with an expert.

"You see, it all happens like this," began Baro Ali after he agreed to sit down with Neil and me and answer our questions. "The men speak the *doware fo* over and over. Then the women are enabled to become pregnant. Pigs have large litters of young. The gardens produce greater amounts of food. The chanting continues until the gardens and pigs are full grown. That's why it takes so long to get ready for the feast. It's the talk that makes everything produce and grow."

I thought about the word *Foke*. It looked as if it came from the words *fo* (talk) and *ke* (something good). In this case the whole feast was about celebrating the people's success at bringing about new life and growth. To put it in a Folopa expression, they "caused everything to become good." If done properly, the effect would last for many years.

At last I could see what I had not seen before—some clues as to the purpose of the feast. The chanting made sense now, even though we never did learn the actual words. We knew what it was intended to do. The *doware fo*, it turned out, was a source of life.

Then it struck me that Neil and I had a parallel purpose in being in this village—to bring the message of life, eternal life. This message came in the form of words—the Word of God. The whole concept of substitutionary sacrifice and a greater life than the one we know now was already well established in the hearts of the Folopa people. Suddenly I thought, *I'm in the right business, bringing the talk that brings new life and growth to a people who might otherwise never have heard it.* I was grateful that we were about halfway through working toward the completion of the Scriptures for these people.

Reflecting on the Papua New Guinean culture, I thought about how all of us as humans try so hard to establish a ritual, make our own rules, then believe we will be rewarded for following them. How vital it is for us to follow the divine pattern in which God gives us life through His Word freely without our having to work for or earn our salvation. No rituals or additional sacrifices are required for us to find life in Jesus Christ. He has already done it all.

Our next trip out of the village was by small airplane. During the years in which we had labored to complete the translation of the New Testament and parts of the Old Testament, the Folopa people had been working on their own long-term project, an airstrip. In 1991 it was completed, dedicated and opened amid great celebration. What a thrill it was to take off and fly out over the area and look down at the landscape that had changed little over the years.

The church was in temporary quarters, waiting for a new and much larger building to be built. The three long, narrow men's houses looked just the same. The women were still living, for the most part, in separate little dwellings lined up on either side of the open area, in front of each of the long houses. The space once occupied by the *temake be,* where many of the *Foke* rituals had been performed, was empty now. The building had been torn down some time back when it was too weak to stand any longer. Then, of course, there were our buildings—our home, the Bible house where some men now helped Neil do the work of Bible translation, and the literacy building.

As we flew over, I thought about the *Foke* feast and what I had been finding out about words that bring life. Once again it was as if my eyes refocused and I saw something I had never noticed before.

The position of the buildings, particularly the long house and the round *temake be*, could likely have been symbols in themselves of sexual reproduction. The names of the buildings even suggested that this was true. The men had told us that the one house was man and the other, woman. I had had no idea what he was talking about, but now I understood.

Not only were the words of chanting bringing life, but other activities as well symbolized the union between the two sexes. The final result of that union was a new birth. In the seclusion of the round *temake be*, the small, buried stones would symbolically grow and be born into the environment. Out in the gardens, plants were bearing fruit in reality.

Looking down, I saw that the men's house no longer pointed to the female *temake be*, as it was gone. Now the long building pointed to the opposite end, to our buildings. It was probably a coincidence that the old symbol was gone and, in a strange way, a new symbol was there—the place where the Word of God was being translated. Did this mean there was still a significant pattern in the village layout?

As this new information sank in, another even greater thought surfaced. God had been using the Folopa people's symbolic religious system to reveal His own much greater truth—the truth about real life. It had been in plain sight all these years, even during my days of struggle and depression. The symbolism was obvious.

On the ground, the modern-day people had somehow lost the deeper meaning of the symbolism, much like those in my American culture who no longer understood our Thanksgiving celebration. Our generation observed the traditions without knowing fully why it was important or where it had come from.

But regardless of the Folopa people's or my abilities to perceive what had been happening over eons of time, God had been at work and had left a sign of His presence. It waited only for us to focus our vision and see what was before us.

God seemed to be saying to me (shades of Martha), *Carol, Carol, you worry about so many things. I have been here working long before you came. I saw what they were doing, trying to find life without Me. I have a plan and I am achieving it. The Folopa people will find life. And just to show you how much I love you, I'm letting you help make it happen.*

Tears streamed down my face as I acknowledged that God had indeed proven to be everything He had said in His Word. I was the one who had worried constantly that I was not worthy of His love. I remembered my anger at Him after my near-death illness when I had turned around and wondered if He was worthy of my love. How foolish I had been ever to doubt, and how foolish to feel angry at Him for letting me down! His ways were not my ways. I would have managed things to make them more comfortable for me and mine. But God had chosen another path—one that led through the storms and fires of life.

He had said through the prophet Isaiah:

> "I am God, and there is no other;
> I am God, and there is none like me.
> I make known the end from the beginning,
>   from ancient times, what is still to come.
> I say: My purpose will stand,
>   and I will do all that I please. . . .
> What I have said, that will I bring about;
>   what I have planned, that will I do."
>   Isaiah 46:9–11

Nothing changes an attitude like a view of the big picture! I knew that the really big picture was even more exciting than this. But just a little view from above was enough to expand my vision.

Dawn of a New Day

The path of the righteous is like the first gleam of dawn, shining ever brighter till the full light of day.

Proverbs 4:18

I opened my eyes to a gray predawn haze. It was Easter Sunday again. Brushing the mosquito net aside, as I did every morning, I rolled out of bed. Would there be a glorious sunrise?

Our bedroom window faced eastward for the very purpose of catching this rare moment. I pulled the curtains aside and observed heavy clouds just at the point where I expected the sun to rise. But the rest of the sky was clear, which usually meant a bright, hot morning. The sunrise would be observable but not spectacular.

Instead of disappointment, I felt a tingle of excitement. The day's events promised to far exceed the joy of a simple weather phenomenon. This was the day Fukutao village had planned for months—the district-wide Easter worship service of the Evangelical Church of Papua.

Outside I heard shouts and the slap of bare feet on soft mud. The church leaders were running here and there putting the final touches on the program. Right below our bedroom window, some young men huddled, "secretly" rehearsing their parts. Was it to be a skit or play? They did not want to reveal the surprise until the last moment.

Before the sun was even up, crowds of visitors to the village started to gather. The excitement in the atmosphere was as dense as the humid air. People had come to participate in the Easter weekend from villages all around the Folopa and neighboring language group areas. The Sunday service would be the most dramatic and elaborate of the almost continual meetings that had started on Friday and were finishing Easter night.

"Heto Ali, Heto Hama." An urgent call from the front door pushed me a little faster to get myself in gear.

"What is it?" I called in return.

"We need more copies of the Bible reading," came the voice again. "More people have come who want to be part of the service."

It was Oliver, one of the men who helped Neil do the work of Bible translation. When we had first arrived, he was a young boy. Now he was married to Hariso, the girl next door, and a valuable member of the team of men who met daily to "turn God's talk" carefully into their mother tongue.

"I'll start printing right away," I answered, heading for my study and the battery-driven computer printer, which had produced hundreds of pages of rough drafts over the years. Slowly but steadily it would now print the last few copies of the chosen Easter readings for the day.

Our little family bustled out the door, carrying our own seating accommodation. We joined others heading in the direction of the open area that had been the site of the original church building—that old building where Neil and I had eaten our lunch on our first visit to Fukutao. It had been torn down, and a new church was in the planning stage. The empty grounds had been enlarged and flattened so that a large crowd could gather, sitting on logs, bark cloth mats and bits of plastic sheeting.

I stood in one spot and looked around in a full, 360-degree turn. We were gathered on top of a bare, open, east-west running ridge. The north and south sides of our "church of the air" fell away steeply so that the only view was of the two parallel mountain ridges across the valleys. A speaker's podium had been erected against the backdrop of the north ridge. As the sun rose slowly in the sky, it sidelighted the jagged peaks and frequent irregularities in the mountain, giving a touch of awesome wonder and enormity to the setting.

The church leaders took their places on the platform, along with a worship team of young people. There were Joshua, Hariso, Futo, Apusi, and several others who had been born about the time Neil and I first came to Fukutao. A hush fell over the crowd as the action began.

Trotting toward us from the western side of the meeting place was the group I had heard earlier practicing under my window. They were all decked out in traditional war paint, feathers, colorful leaves and animal fur, and equipped with spears and bark shields. These, too, had been decorated for the occasion in painted designs that had been used for untold generations.

They broke into two opposing groups and faced each other, hopping from one foot to the other and chanting the old war chants in unison. Soon they were thrusting spears toward one another in mock battle, trying to make their performance look as authentic as possible. Two men fell and lay motionless on the ground.

On the sidelines the women began to mourn loudly. The men, particularly of the older generation, shook their heads from side to side and grieved with the crowd. The memories were still strong. I cried with them as they played out the scene from the days of old that were not that far in the past.

Then a lone figure walked slowly between the crowd and the shouting warriors. He was carrying a heavy crossed log. Dragging it to the east side of the clearing, he and some other actors planted it in a hole in the ground. The others, wearing hats of various kinds and reed skirts over their clothing representing the attire of Roman soldiers, managed to get the lone figure positioned up on the cross to simulate a crucifixion.

Suddenly the battle was over. The fighters bowed their heads as if in shame and walked over to the crucifixion scene, laying their spears and shields down at the base of the cross. They bowed deeply, along with the soldiers, while the congregation continued to weep and mourn, now for the sacrificed Christ.

The worship team leader began to sing in English, his voice cracking with emotion:

> Lord, we lift Your name on high;
> Lord, we love to sing Your praises;
> We're so glad You're in our life;
> We're so glad You came to save us.
> You came from heaven to earth to show the way,
> From the earth to the cross my debt to pay,
> From the cross to the grave, from the grave to the sky
> Lord, we lift Your name on high.

The pastor stood to speak.

"We are a people who have had a dark past. When someone tried to kill one of us, we thought only of our hatred and of getting revenge. We fought, as these men have fought this morning, only to kill and bring more killing from that killing.

"Then we followed our customs and performed the rituals to cleanse ourselves from evil and to bring life from the death that was all around us. We worked hard to make ourselves pleasing to the spirit world so they would do no more harm to us. But in the end were only more sorrow and pain. We could not please the spirits, nor the gods of this world.

"Then came the news that God, the Creator, had made a way. A sacrificial death had become the substitute for us. This death did not merely distract God from paying us back for our bad ways; it paid for all of them. There would be no more payback from an angry God, but instead love from Him. This God did the unheard-of: He gave His only Son to be that sacrifice."

The pastor gestured toward the figure still hanging on the cross.

"Jesus Christ did not stay in the grave," he continued, "as all the bodies we have buried have done. He came back to life to prove that He could give us life. Today we celebrate because we can have that kind of powerful life force in us. It does not come from the spirits; it comes from God in Jesus Christ."

The service concluded with several testimonies, another sermon from a visiting pastor and Folopa church songs.

Standing in the clearing after the crowd had dispersed, gazing off to the southern ridges, I remembered my first helicopter landing on this spot years before. A young man had said, "You come back," so we did. The verse from Isaiah 55 crossed my mind: "You will go out in joy and be led forth in peace; the mountains and hills will burst into song before you, and all the trees of the field will clap their hands."

Perhaps I had mistakenly thought this meant my experience would be easy. No, it had certainly not been easy. But in light of all that God planned to do in this place, it was a prophetic promise.

I remembered the next arrival, when I had stayed for several months, looking into the faces of these strange people and asking myself if the Lord was going to keep His promises. I had wondered if I would be accepted by the Folopa people and if I would perform adequately in this difficult calling. What would happen if I failed? Would God be disappointed in me or abandon me?

Now I knew the answers. Yes, He would keep His promises. Yes, He would use me despite my weaknesses and failings. Yes, He would accept me and love me no matter what I did or did not do in my service to Him. As the pastor had said in his moving sermon that morning, I could not expect to earn God's love by keeping a list of rules or by performing religious rituals. He had given His love freely and unconditionally. And none of us, including me, was beyond God's reach or His ability to save.

Standing on the ridge with the wind blowing in my face and the rain-laden clouds pouring in over the southern mountains, I remembered the promise He had given me when I prayed for direction about what language group to work in:

"As the rain and the snow
   come down from heaven,
and do not return to it
   without watering the earth
and making it bud and flourish,
   so that it yields seed for the sower and bread for the
      eater,
so is my word that goes out from my mouth:
   It will not return to me empty,
but will accomplish what I desire
   and achieve the purpose for which I sent it."
                        Isaiah 55:10–11

God's Word had brought life to this village in Papua New Guinea, with seeds planted long ago and with the watering of truth that brings plants to life out of the dry ground.

His Word had brought life to me as well. In it I had learned who God really was and what He had done for me. His love and grace had been poured out freely. God really did know after all what He was doing!

With joy in my heart, I started down the ridge.